D0469994

Woman, Thou Art Loosed!

BISHOP T.D. JAKES

© Copyright 1993 - Bishop T.D. Jakes

All rights reserved. This book is protected under the copyright laws of the United States of America. This book may not be copied or reprinted for commercial gain or profit. The use of short quotations or occasional page copying for personal or group study is permitted and encouraged. Permission will be granted upon request. Unless otherwise identified, Scripture quotations are from the King James Version of the Bible.

Take note that the name satan and related names are not capitalized. We choose not to acknowledge him, even to the point of violating grammatical rules.

Treasure House
An Imprint of
Destiny Image® Publishers, Inc.
P.O. Box 310
Shippensburg, PA 17257-0310

"For where your treasure is,
there will your heart be also." Matthew 6:21

ISBN 0-7684-2289-2
(Previously published under ISBN 0-7684-3040-2)
For Worldwide Distribution
Printed in the U.S.A.

2 3 4 5 6 7 8 9 10 11 12 13/10 09 08 07 06 05

This book and all other Destiny Image, Revival Press, MercyPlace, Fresh Bread, Destiny Image Fiction, and Treasure House books are available at Christian bookstores and distributors worldwide.

For a U.S. bookstore nearest you, call **1-800-722-6774**.
For more information on foreign distributors, call **717-532-3040**.
Or reach us on the Internet:
www.destinyimage.com

DEDICATION

I want to dedicate this book to the memory of my father, the late Rev. Ernest L. Jakes, Sr. Dedicated to my father, it is also in tribute to my mother, Mrs. Odith P. Jakes, whose unfailing love has defined motherhood and was my first encounter with excellence. To my sister, Jackie, who kissed away my childhood tears and finally to my lovely wife, Serita, whose gentle breeze has often kept my sails full of the wind of destiny.

About the Book

Woman, Thou Art Loosed is the heart of the Father ministering to the women of His Son's Body. Literally thousands of women have been set free by the anointed word of T.D. Jakes. It's mind-challenging, life-changing and spirit-transforming truth. Your life will never be the same after reading this book.

Pastor Carlton Pearson
Higher Dimensions Inc.
Tulsa, Okla.

Every woman in this country needs to hear the message that God has given Bishop Jakes. It is impossible for someone to hear this message and not be encouraged, delivered and transformed forever. I know that because of this word from God, my life will never be the same.

Dr. Debbye Turner
Miss America 1990
St. Louis, Mo.

v

Our church, The Center of Hope, in Oakland, California, has been greatly impacted by this man's ministry. I want to highly recommend *Woman, Thou Art Loosed* to every woman in this country. You will be blessed!

Dr. Ernestine Cleveland Reems
President, E.C. Reems Women's
International Ministries
and Founding Pastor
Center of Hope, Oakland, Calif.

CONTENTS

Chapter 1

INFIRMED WOMAN

And, behold, there was a woman which had a spirit of infirmity eighteen years, and was bowed together, and could in no wise lift up herself. And when Jesus saw her, He called her to Him, and said unto her, Woman, thou art loosed from thine infirmity. Luke 13:11-12

The Holy Spirit periodically lets us catch a glimpse of the personal testimony of one of the patients of the Divine Physician Himself. This woman's dilemma is her own, but perhaps you will find some point of relativity between her case history and your own. She could be like someone you know or have known; she could even be like you.

There are three major characters in this story. These characters are the person, the problem and the prescription. It is important to remember that for every person, there will be a problem. Even more importantly, for every problem, our God has a prescription!

Jesus' opening statement to the problem in this woman's life is not a recommendation for counseling—it is a challenging command! Often much more is involved in maintaining deliverance than just discussing past trauma. Jesus did not counsel what should have been commanded. I am not, however, against seeking the counsel of godly men. On the contrary, the Scriptures say:

> *Blessed is the man that walketh not in the counsel of the ungodly, nor standeth in the way of sinners, nor sitteth in the seat of the scornful.* Psalm 1:1

> *Where no counsel is, the people fall: but in the multitude of counsellors there is safety.* Proverbs 11:14

What I want to make clear is that after you have analyzed the condition, after you have understood its origin, it will still take the authority of God's Word to put the past under your feet! This woman was suffering as a result of something that attacked her 18 years earlier. I wonder if you can relate to the long-range aftereffects of past pain? This kind of trauma is as fresh to the victim today as it was the day it occurred. Although the problem may be rooted in the past, the prescription is a present word from God! The Word is the same yesterday, today and forevermore! (Heb. 13:8) That is to say, the word you are hearing today is able to heal your yesterday!

Jesus said, "Woman, thou art loosed." He did not call her by name. He wasn't speaking to her just as a person. He spoke to her femininity. He spoke to the song in her. He spoke to the lace in her. Like a crumbling rose, Jesus spoke to what she could, and would, have been. I believe the Lord spoke to the twinkle that existed in her eye when she was a child; to the girlish glow that makeup can never seem to recapture. He spoke to her God-given uniqueness. He spoke to her gender.

Her problem didn't begin suddenly. It had existed in her life for 18 years. We are looking at a woman who had a personal war going on inside her. These struggles must have tainted many other areas of her life. The infirmity that attacked her life was physical. However, many women also wrestle with infirmities in emotional traumas. These infirmities can be just as challenging as a physical affliction. An emotional handicap can create dependency on many different levels. Relationships can become crutches. The infirmed woman then places such weight on people that it stresses a healthy relationship. Many times such emotional handicaps will spawn a series of unhealthy relationships.

For thou hast had five husbands; and he whom thou now hast is not thy husband: in that saidst thou truly. John 4:18

Healing cannot come to a desperate person rummaging through other people's lives. One of the first things that a hurting person needs to do is break the habit of using other people as a narcotic to numb the dull aching of an inner void. The more you medicate the symptoms,

3

the less chance you have of allowing God to heal you. The other destructive tendency that can exist with any abuse is the person must keep increasing the dosage. Avoid addictive, obsessive relationships. If you are becoming increasingly dependent upon anything other than God to create a sense of wholeness in your life, then you are abusing your relationships. Clinging to people is far different from loving them. It is not so much a statement of your love for them as it is a crying out of your need for them. Like lust, it is intensely selfish. It is taking and not giving. Love is giving. God is love. God proved His love not by His need of us, but by His giving to us.

> For God so loved the world, that He gave His only begotten Son, that whosoever believeth in Him should not perish, but have everlasting life. John 3:16

The Scriptures plainly show that this infirmed woman had tried to lift herself. People who stand on the outside can easily criticize and assume that the infirmed woman lacks effort and fortitude. That is not always the case. Some situations in which we can find ourselves defy will power. We feel unable to change. The Scriptures say that she "could in no wise lift up herself." That implies she had employed various means of self-ministry. Isn't it amazing how the same people who lift up countless others, often cannot lift themselves? This type of person may be a tower of faith and prayer for others, but impotent when it comes to her own limitations. That person may be the one others rely upon. Sometimes we esteem others more important than ourselves. We always become the martyr. It is wonderful to be self-sacrificing but watch out for self-disdain! If we don't apply some of the medicine that we use on others to strengthen ourselves, our patients will be healed and we will be dying.

> *I shall not die, but live, and declare the works of the Lord.* Psalm 118:17

Many things can engender disappointment and depression. In this woman's case, a spirit of infirmity had gripped her life. A spirit can manifest itself in many forms. For some it may be low self-esteem caused by child abuse, rape, wife abuse or divorce. I realize that these are natural problems, but they are rooted in spiritual ailments. One of the many damaging things that can affect us today is divorce, particularly among women, who often look forward to a happy relationship. Little girls grow up playing with Barbie and Ken dolls, dressing doll babies and playing house. Young girls lie in bed reading romance novels, while little boys play ball and ride bicycles in the park. Whenever a woman is indoctrinated to think success is romance and then experiences the trauma of a failed relationship, she comes to a painful awakening. Divorce is not merely separating; it is the tearing apart of what was once joined together. Whenever something is torn, it does not heal easily. But Jesus can heal a broken or torn heart!

> *The Spirit of the Lord is upon Me, because He hath anointed Me to preach the gospel to the poor; He hath sent Me to heal the brokenhearted, to preach deliverance to the captives, and recovering of sight to the blind, to set at liberty them that are bruised.* Luke 4:18

Approximately five out of ten marriages end in divorce. Those broken homes leave a trail of broken dreams, people and children. Only the Master can heal these victims in the times in which we live. He can treat the long-term effects of this tragedy. One of the great healing balms of the Holy Spirit is forgiveness. To forgive is to break the link between you and your past. Sadly enough, many times the person hardest to forgive is the one in the mirror. Although they rage loudly about others, people secretly blame themselves for a failed relationship. Regardless of who you hold responsible, there is no healing in blame! When you begin to realize that your past does not necessarily dictate the outcome of your future, then you can release the hurt. It is impossible to inhale new air until you exhale the old. I pray that as you continue reading, God would give the grace of releasing where you have been so you can receive what God has for you now. Exhale, then inhale; there is more for you.

Perhaps one of the more serious indictments against our civilization is our flagrant disregard for the welfare of our children. Child abuse, regardless of whether it is physical, sexual or emotional, is a terrible issue for an innocent mind to wrestle with. It is horrifying to think that little children who survive the peril of the streets, the public schools and the aggravated society in which we live, come home to be abused in what should be a haven. Recent statistics suggest that three in five young girls in this country have been or will be sexually assaulted. If that many are reported, I shudder to think of those that never are reported but are covered with a shroud of secrecy.

If by chance you are a pastor, please realize that these figures are actually faces in your choir, committees, etc. They reflect a growing amount of our congregational needs. Although this book focuses on women, many men also have been abused as children. I fear that God will judge us for our blatant disregard of this need in our messages, ministries and prayers. I even would suggest that our silence contributes to the shame and secrecy that satan attaches to these victimized persons. Whenever I think on these issues, I am reminded of what my mother used to say. I was forever coming home with a scratch or cut from schoolyard play. My mother would take the band-aid off, clean the wound and say, "Things that are covered don't heal well." Mother was right. Things that are covered do not heal well.

Perhaps Jesus was thinking on this order when He called the infirmed woman to come forward. It takes a lot of courage even in church today to receive ministry in sensitive areas. The Lord, though, is the kind of physician who can pour on the healing oil. Uncover your wounds in His presence and allow Him to gently heal the injuries. One woman found healing in the hem of His garment (Mk. 5:25-29). There is a balm in Gilead! (Jer. 8:22)

Even when the victim survives, there is still a casualty. It is the death of trust. Surely you realize that little girls tend to be trusting and unsuspicious. When those who should nurture and protect them violate that trust through illicit behavior, multiple scars result. It is like programming a computer with false information; you can get out of it only what has been programmed into it. When a man tells a little girl that his perverted acts are normal, she has no reason not to believe that what she is being taught is true. She is devoted to him, allowing him to fondle her or further misappropriate his actions toward her. Usually the abuser is someone very close, with access to the child at vulnerable times. Fear is also a factor, as many children lay down with the cold taste of fear in their mouths. They believe he could and would kill them for divulging his liberties against them. Some, as the victims of rape, feel physically powerless to wrestle with the assailant.

What kind of emotions might this kind of conduct bring out in the later life of this person? I am glad you asked. It would be easy for this kind of little girl to grow into a young lady who has difficulty trusting anyone! Maybe she learns to deal with the pain inside by getting attention in illicit ways. Drug rehabilitation centers and prisons are full of adults who were abused children needing attention.

Not every abused child takes such drastic steps. Often their period of behavioral disorder dissipates with time. However, the abused child struggles with her own self-worth. She reasons, "How can I be valuable if the only way I could please my own father was to have sex with him?" This kind of childhood can affect how later relationships progress. Intimidated by intimacy, she struggles with trusting anyone. Insecurity and jealousy may be constant companions to this lady, who can't seem to grasp the idea that someone could love her. There are a variety of reactions as varied as there are individuals. Some avoid people who really care, being attracted to those who do not treat them well. Relating to abuse, they seem to sabotage good relationships and struggle for years in worthless ones. Still others may be emotionally incapacitated to the degree that they need endless affirmation and affection just to maintain the courage to face ordinary days.

The pastor may tell this lady that God is her heavenly Father. That doesn't help, because the problem is her point of reference. We frame our references around our own experiences. If those experiences are distorted, our ability to comprehend spiritual truths can be off center. I know that may sound very negative for someone who is in that circumstance. What do you do when you have been poorly programmed by life's events? I've got good news! You can re-program your mind through the Word of God.

> *Do not conform any longer to the pattern of this world, but be transformed by the renewing of your mind. Then you will be able to test and approve what God's will is—His good, pleasing and perfect will.* Romans 12:2 (NIV)

The Greek word metamorphôō is translated as "transformed" in this text. Literally, it means to change into another form! You can have a complete metamorphosis through the Word of God. It has been my experience as a pastor who does extensive counseling in my own ministry and abroad, that many abused people, women in particular, tend to flock to legalistic churches who see God primarily as a disciplinarian. Many times the concept of fatherhood for them is a harsh code of ethics. This type of domineering ministry may appeal to those who are performance-oriented. I understand that morality is important in Christianity; however, there is a great deal of difference between morality and legalism. It is important that God not be misrepresented. He is a balanced God, not an extremist.

> *The Word became flesh and made His dwelling among us. We have seen His glory, the glory of the One and Only, who came from the Father, full of grace and truth.* John 1:14 (NIV)

The glory of God is manifested only when there is a balance between grace and truth. Religion doesn't transform. Legalism doesn't transform. For the person who feels dirty, harsh rules could create a sense of self-righteousness. God doesn't have to punish you to heal you. Jesus has already prayed for you.

> *Sanctify them through Thy truth: Thy word is truth.* John 17:17

Jesus simply shared grace and truth with that hurting woman. He said, "Woman, thou art loosed." Believe the Word of God and be free. Jesus our Lord was a great emancipator of the oppressed. It does not matter whether someone has been oppressed socially, sexually or racially; our Lord is an eliminator of distinctions.

> *There is neither Jew nor Greek* [racial], *there is neither bond nor free* [social], *there is neither male nor female* [sexual]: *for ye are all one in Christ Jesus.* Galatians 3:28

I feel it is important to point out that this verse deals with unity and equality in regard to the covenant of salvation. That is to say, God is no respecter of persons. He tears down barriers that would promote prejudice and separation in the Body of Christ. Yet it is important also to note that while there is no distinction in the manner in which we receive any of those groups, there should be an appreciation for the uniqueness of the groups' individuality. There is a racial, social and sexual uniqueness that we should not only accept, but also appreciate. It is cultural rape to teach other cultures or races that the only way to worship God is the way another race or culture does. Unity should not come at the expense of uniqueness of expression. We should also tolerate variance in social classes. It is wonderful to teach prosperity as long as it is understood that the Church is not an elite organization for spiritual yuppies only, one that excludes other social classes.

If uniqueness is to be appreciated racially and socially, it is certainly to be appreciated sexually. Male and female are one in Christ. Yet they are unique and that uniqueness is not to be tampered with. Let the male be masculine and the female be feminine! It is a sin for a man to misrepresent himself by conducting himself as a woman. I am not merely speaking of homosexuality. I am also talking about men who are feminine in their mannerisms. Many of these men may not be homosexual in their behavior, but the Bible says that they must be healed of feminine mannerisms, or vice versa. It is equally sad to see a masculine woman. Nevertheless, God wants them healed, not hated!

> *Know ye not that the unrighteous shall not*
> *inherit the kingdom of God? Be not deceived:*
> *neither fornicators, nor idolaters, nor adulter-*
> *ers, nor effeminate, nor abusers of themselves*
> *with mankind....* 1 Corinthians 6:9

Strong's #3120 "*malakos* (mal-ak-os'); of uncertain
affinity; soft, i.e. fine (clothing); figuratively, a
catamite:—effeminate, soft" (*Strong's Exhaus-*
tive Concordance of the Bible, Hendrickson
Publishers, n.d.).

I realize that these behavioral disorders are areas that
require healing and prayer. My point is simply that unity
does not negate uniqueness. God is saying, "I don't want
men to lose their masculine uniqueness." This is true
racially, socially and sexually. God can appreciate our dif-
ferences and still create unity. It is like a conductor who
can orchestrate extremely different instruments into producing a harmonious, unified sound. Together we produce a sound of harmony that expresses the multifaceted
character of God.

Having established the uniqueness of unity, let us
now discuss some aspects of the uniqueness of the
woman. By nature a woman is a receiver. She is not physically designed to be a giver. Her sexual and emotional
fulfillment becomes somewhat dependent on the giving
of her male counterpart (in regard to intimate relationships). There is a certain vulnerability that is a part of
being a receiver. In regard to reproduction (sexual relationships), the man is the contributing factor, and the
woman is the receiver.

What is true of the natural is true of the spiritual. Men tend to act out of what they perceive to be facts, while women tend to react out of their emotions. If your actions and moods are not a reaction to the probing of the Holy Spirit, then you are reacting to the subtle taunting of the enemy. He is trying to produce his destructive fruit in your home, heart, and even in your relationships. Receiver, be careful what you receive! Moods and attitudes that satan would offer, you need to resist. Tell the enemy, "This is not me, and I don't receive it." It is his job to offer it and your job to resist it. If you do your job, all will go well.

> *Submit yourselves, then, to God. Resist the devil, and he will flee from you.* James 4:7 (NIV)

Don't allow the enemy to plug into you and violate you through his subtle seductions. He is a giver and he is looking for a receiver. You must discern his influence if you are going to rebuke him. Anything that comes, any mood that is not in agreement with God's Word, is satan trying to plug into the earthly realm through your life. He wants you to believe you cannot change. He loves prisons and chains! Statements like, "This is just the way I am," or "I am in a terrible mood today," come from lips that accept what they ought to reject. Never allow yourself to settle for anything less than the attitude God wants you to have in your heart. Don't let satan have your day, your husband or your home. Eve could have put the devil out!

Neither give place to the devil. Ephesians 4:27

It is not enough to reject the enemy's plan. You must nurture the Word of the Lord. You need to draw the promise of God and the vision for the future to your breast. It is a natural law that anything not fed will die. Whatever you have drawn to the breast is what is growing in your life. Breast-feeding holds several advantages for what you feed: (a) It hears your heart beat; (b) it is warmed by your closeness; (c) it draws nourishment from you. Caution: Be sure you are nurturing what you want to grow and starving what you want to die.

As you read this, you may feel that life is passing you by. You often experience success in one area and gross defeat in others. You need a burning desire for the future, the kind of desire that overcomes past fear and inhibitions. You will remain chained to your past and all the secrets therein until you decide: Enough is enough! I am telling you that when your desire for the future peaks, you can break out of prison. I challenge you to sit down and write 30 things you would like to do with your life and scratch them off, one by one, as you accomplish them. There is no way you can plan for the future and dwell in the past at the same time. I feel an earthquake coming into your prison! It is midnight—the turning point of days! It is your time for a change. Praise God and escape out of the dungeons of your past.

And at midnight Paul and Silas prayed, and
sang praises unto God: and the prisoners heard
them. And suddenly there was a great earth-
quake, so that the foundations of the prison
were shaken: and immediately all the doors

were opened, and every one's bands were
loosed. Acts 16:25-26

Have you ever noticed how hard it is to communicate with people who will not give you their attention? Pain will not continue to rehearse itself in the life of a preoccupied, distracted person. Distracted people almost seem weird. They do not respond! Every woman has something she wishes she could forget. There is a principle to learn here. Forgetting isn't a memory lapse; it is a memory release! Like carbon dioxide the body can no longer use, exhale it and let it go out of your spirit.

Brethren, I count not myself to have appre-
hended: but this one thing I do, forgetting
those things which are behind, and reaching
forth unto those things which are before, I
press toward the mark for the prize of the high
calling of God in Christ Jesus. Let us therefore,
as many as be perfect, be thus minded: and if
in any thing ye be otherwise minded, God shall
reveal even this unto you. Philippians 3:13-15

Jesus set the infirmed woman free. She was able to stand upright. The crippling condition of her infirmity was removed by the God who cares, sees and calls the infirmity to the dispensary of healing and deliverance. You can call upon Him even in the middle of the night. Like a 24-hour medical center, you can reach Him at anytime. He is touched by the feeling of your infirmity.

For we have not an high priest which cannot be
touched with the feeling of our infirmities; but

*was in all points tempted like as we are, yet
without sin.* Hebrews 4:15

*In the name of our High Priest, Jesus Christ, I curse
the infirmity that has bowed the backs of God's women.* I
pray that, as we share together out of the Word of God,
the Holy Spirit would roll you into the recovery room
where you can fully realize that the trauma is over. I am
excited to say that God never loosed anybody that He
wasn't going to use mightily. May God reveal healing and
purpose as we continue to seek Him.

Chapter 2

BROKEN ARROWS

*Lo, children are an heritage of the Lord: and
the fruit of the womb is His reward. As arrows
are in the hand of a mighty man; so are children of the youth. Happy is the man that hath
his quiver full of them: they shall not be
ashamed, but they shall speak with the enemies in the gate. Psalm 127:3-5*

The birth of a child is still the greatest miracle I have
ever seen. Standing in the sterile white environment of a
hospital maternity ward with the smell of disinfectant
strong on my hands like a strange new cologne, they just
handed me my link into the future, my ambassador to the
next generation. Blinking, winking, squirming little slice
of love, wrapped in a blanket and forever fastened to my
heart—we had just had a baby! To me a piece of Heaven
had been pushed through the womb of our consummat-
ed love. Children are living epistles that should stand as

evidence to the future that the past made some level of contribution.

The psalmist David wrote a brief note that is as loud as an atomic bomb. It speaks to the heart of men about their attitude toward their offspring. This was David, the man whose indiscretion with Bathsheba had produced a love child. Though inappropriately conceived, the baby was loved nonetheless. David is the man who laid upon the ground in sackcloth and ashes praying feverishly for mercy as his child squirmed in the icy hands of death. Somewhere in a tent the cold silence slowly grew. The squirming stopped, the crying stilled; the baby has gone into eternal rest. If anybody knows the value of children, it is those who just left theirs in the ground. "As arrows are in the hand of a mighty man; so are children of the youth," says King David whose arrow they lowered in the ground.

Why did he compare children to arrows? Maybe it was for their potential to be propelled into the future. Perhaps it was for the intrinsic gold mine that lies in the heart of every child who is shot through the womb. Maybe he was trying to tell us that children go where we, their parents, aim them. Could it be that we, as parents, must be responsible enough to place them in the kind of bow that will accelerate their success and emotional well-being? How happy I am to have a quiver full of arrows.

If someone must be hurt, if it ever becomes necessary to bear pains, weather strong winds, or withstand trials or opposition, let it be adults and not children. Whatever happens, happens. I can accept the fate before me. I was my father's arrow and my mother's heart. My father is dead, but his arrows are yet soaring in the wind. You will never know him; he is gone. However, my brother, my sister, and I are flying, soaring, scientific proof that he was, and through us, continues to be. So don't worry about me; I am an arrow shot. If I don't succeed, I have had the greatest riches known to man. I have had an opportunity to test the limits of my destiny. Whether preferred or rejected, let the record show: I am here. Oh, God, let me hit my target! But if I miss and plummet to the ground, then at least I can say, "I have been shot!"

It is for the arrows of this generation that we must pray—they who are being aimed at the streets and drugs and perversion. Not all of them, but some of them have been broken in the quiver! I write to every empty-eyed child I have ever seen sit at my desk with tears and trembling lips struggling to tell the unmentionable secret. I write to the trembling voice of every caller who spoke into a telephone a secret they could not keep and could not tell. I write to every husband who holds a woman every night, a child lost in space, a rosebud crushed before you met her, a broken arrow shaking in the quiver. I write to every lady who hides behind silk dresses and leather purses a terrible secret that makeup can't seem to cover and long showers will not wash. Some people call them abused children. Some call them victimized. Some call them statistics. But I call them broken arrows.

Whose hand is this that fondles the bare, flat chest of a little girl? Whose fingers linger upon the flesh he helped to create? Why has the love that should be mama's come to snuggle under daughter? "Someone tell me how to rinse the feeling of fingers off my mind?" This is the cry of little children all over this country. This is the cry of worried minds clutching dolls, riding bicycles—little girls and even little boys sitting on school buses who got more for Christmas than they could ever show and tell. The Church must realize that the adult problems we are fighting to correct are often rooted in the ashes of childhood experiences.

How delicate is the touch of a surgeon's hand. Who needs surgery under a butchering hack saw? In the ministry, there is a different prerequisite for effectiveness than what the textbooks alone can provide. It is not a medicine compiled by a pharmacist that is needed for the patients lying on the tables of my heart. We don't need medicine; we need miracles. I always laugh at the carnal mind that picks up books like this to critique the approach of the prophet. They weigh the words of divine wisdom against the data they have studied. Many have more faith in a textbook written by a person whose eyes may be clouded by their own secrets, than to rely upon the word of a God who knows the end from the beginning. Whatever the psychologist learned, he read it in a book, heard it in a lecture, or discovered it in an experiment. I appreciate the many who have been helped through these precious hearts. Yet I know that, at best, we are practicing an uncertain method on people as we ramble through the closets of a troubled person's mind. We need divine intervention!

If there is something minor wrong with my car, like a radiator hose needing replaced or a tire changed, I can take it almost anywhere. But if I suspect there is serious trouble with it, I always take it to the dealer.

The manufacturer knows his product better than the average mechanic. So like the dealership, ministers may work with, but need not be intimidated by, the sciences of the mind! God is not practicing. He is accomplished. I want to share God-given, biblical answers to troubling questions as we deal with the highly sensitive areas of sexually abused children.

I earnestly believe that where there is no compassion, there can be no lasting change. As long as Christian leadership secretly jeers and sneers at the perversion that comes into the Church, there will be no healing. Perversion is the offspring of abuse! As long as we crush what is already broken by our own prejudices and phobias, there will be no healing. The enemy robs us of our healing power by robbing us of our concern.

Compassion is the mother of miracles! When the storm had troubled the waters and Peter thought he would die, he didn't challenge Christ's power; he challenged His compassion. He went into the back of the ship and said, "Carest Thou not that we perish?" (Mk. 4:38) He understood that if there is no real compassion, then there can be no miracle. Until we, as priests, are touched with the feelings of our parishioners' illnesses rather than just turned off by their symptoms, they will not be healed. To every husband who wants to see his wife healed, to every mother who has a little girl with a woman's problem: The power to heal is in the power to care. If you are a broken arrow, please allow someone into the storm. I know you usually do not allow anyone to come to your aid. I realize a breach of trust may have left you leery of everyone, but the walls you built to protect you have also imprisoned you. The Lord wants to loose you out of the dungeon of fear. He does care. We care. No one would take hours away from themselves and from their family praying for you, preaching to you, or even writing this to you if they didn't care. *Rise and be healed in the name of Jesus.*

What happened to Peter? Jesus rebuked him! How could he have thought that the God who rode with him in the storm didn't care about the storm? Jesus said, "Peace, be still" (Mk. 4:39). To you He is still saying, "Peace, be still!"

> *But when He saw the multitudes, He was moved with compassion on them, because they fainted, and were scattered abroad, as sheep having no shepherd.* Matthew 9:36

> *And Jesus went forth, and saw a great multitude, and was moved with compassion toward them, and He healed their sick.* Matthew 14:14

> *Then the lord of that servant was moved with compassion, and loosed him, and forgave him the debt.* Matthew 18:27

> *And Jesus, moved with compassion, put forth His hand, and touched him, and saith unto him, I will; be thou clean.* Mark 1:41

> *And Jesus, when He came out, saw much people, and was moved with compassion toward them, because they were as sheep not having a*

shepherd: and He began to teach them many things. Mark 6:34

Preceding miracle after miracle, compassion provoked power. We can build all the churches we want. We can decorate them with fine tapestry and ornate artifacts, but if people cannot find a loving voice within our hallowed walls, they will pass through unaltered by our clichés and religious rhetoric. We can no longer ostracize the victim and let the assailant escape! Every time you see some insecure, vulnerable, intimidated adult who has unnatural fear in her eyes, low self-esteem or an apologetic posture, she is saying, "Carest thou not that I perish?" Every time you see a bra-less woman in men's jeans, choosing to act like a man rather than to sleep with one; every time you see a handsome young man who could have been someone's father, walking like someone's mother—you may be looking child abuse in the face. If you think it's ugly, you're right. If you think it's wrong, you're right again. If you think it can't be healed, you're dead wrong! If you look closely into these eyes I've so feebly tried to describe, you will sense that something in this person is weak, hurt, maimed or disturbed, but fixable.

These splintered, broken arrows come in all colors and forms. Some are black, some white; some are rich, some poor. One thing about pain, though: It isn't prejudiced. Often camouflaged behind the walls of otherwise successful lives, people wrestle with secret pain. We must not narrow the scope of our ministries. Many people bear no outward signs of trauma as dramatic as I have described. Yet there are tragedies severe enough to have destroyed their lives had God not held them together. To God be the glory. He is a magnificent Healer!

Each person who has been through these adversities has her own story. Some have been blessed by not having to experience any such circumstance. Let the strong bear the infirmities of the weak. God can greatly use you to restore wholeness to others who walk in varying degrees of brokenness. After all, every car accident doesn't have the same assessment of damage. Many people have sustained injury without submitting to the ineffective narcotics of sinful and often perverted life styles. But to those who have fallen prey to satan's snares, we teach righteousness while still loving the unrighteous. Most of us have had some degree of cracking, tearing or damage. The fact that we have persevered is a testimony to all who understand themselves to be broken arrows.

> *And they brought young children to Him, that*
> *He should touch them: and His disciples*
> *rebuked those that brought them. But when*
> *Jesus saw it, He was much displeased, and said*
> *unto them, Suffer the little children to come*
> *unto Me, and forbid them not: for of such is the*
> *kingdom of God. Verily I say unto you,*
> *Whosoever shall not receive the kingdom of*
> *God as a little child, he shall not enter therein.*
> *And He took them up in His arms, put His*
> *hands upon them, and blessed them.*
> Mark 10:13-16

It is interesting to me that just before this took place the Lord was ministering on the subject of divorce and adultery. When He brought up that subject, someone brought the children to Him so He could touch them. Broken homes often produce broken children. These little ones are often caught in the cross fire of angry parents. It reminds me of a newscast report on the Gulf War. It was a listing of the many young men who were accidentally killed by their own military—killed, however innocently, in the confusion of the battle. The newscaster used a term I had not heard before. He called it "friendly fire." I thought, *What is friendly about bleeding to death with your face buried in the hot sun of a strange country? I mean, it doesn't help much when I am dead!* Many children are wounded in the friendly fire of angry parents.

Who were these nameless persons who had the insight and the wisdom to bring the children to the Master? They brought the children to Him that He might touch them. What a strange interruption to a discourse on adultery and divorce. Here are these little children dragging dirty blankets and blank gazes into the presence of a God who is dealing with grown-up problems. He takes time from His busy schedule not so much to counsel them, but just to touch them. That's all it takes. I salute all the wonderful people who work with children. Whether through children's church or public school, you have a very high calling. Don't forget to touch their little lives with a word of hope and a smile of encouragement. It may be the only one some will receive. You are the builders of our future. Be careful, for you may be building a house that we will have to live in!

What is wrong with these disciples that they became angry at some nameless person who aimed these little arrows at the only answer they might ever have gotten to see? Who told them they were too busy to heal their own children? Jesus stopped teaching on the cause of divorce and marital abuse to touch the victim, to minister to the effect of the abuse. He told them to suffer the little children to come. Suffer the suffering to come! It is hard to work with hurting people, but the time has come for us to suffer the suffering to come. Anything, whether an injured animal or a hospital patient, if it is hurt, is unhappy. We cannot get a wounded lion to jump through hoops! Hurting children as well as hurting adults can carry the unpleasant aroma of bitterness. In spite of the challenge, it is foolish to give up on your own. So they brought the "ouch" to the band-aid, and He stopped His message for His mission. Imagine tiny hands outstretched, little faces upturned, perching like sparrows on His knee. They came to get a touch, but He always gives us more than we expected. He held them with His loving arms. He touched with His sensitive hands. But most of all, He blessed them with His compassionate heart!

I am concerned that we maintain our compassion. How can we be in the presence of a loving God and then not love little ones? When Jesus blessed the children, He challenged the adults to become as children. Oh, to be a child again, to allow ourselves the kind of relationship with God that we may have missed as a child. Sometimes we need to allow the Lord to adjust the damaged places of our past. I am glad to say that God provides arms that allow grown children to climb up like children and be nurtured through the tragedies of early days. Isn't it nice to toddle into the presence of God and let Him hold you in His arms? In God, we can become children again. Salvation is God giving us a chance to start over again. He will not abuse the children that come to Him. Through praise, I approach Him like a toddler on unskillful legs. In worship, I kiss His face and am held by the caress of His anointing. He has no ulterior motive, for His caress is safe and wholesome. It is so important that we learn how to worship and adore Him. There is no better way to climb into His arms. Even if you were exposed to grown-up situations when you were a child, God can reverse what you've been through. He'll let the grown-up person experience the joy of being a child in the presence of God!

> Because thou shalt forget thy misery, and
> remember it as waters that pass away: and
> thine age shall be clearer than the noonday;
> thou shalt shine forth, thou shalt be as the
> morning. And thou shalt be secure, because
> there is hope; yea, thou shalt dig about thee,
> and thou shalt take thy rest in safety. Also thou
> shalt lie down, and none shall make thee
> afraid; yea, many shall make suit unto thee.
> Job 11:16-19

It is inconceivable to the injured that the injury can be forgotten. However, as I mentioned in the first chapter, to forget isn't to develop amnesia. It is to reach a place where the misery is pulled from the memory as a stinger pulled out of an insect bite. Once the stinger is gone, healing is inevitable. This passage points out so eloquently that the memory is as "waters that pass away." Stand in a stream with waters around your ankles. The waters that pass by you at that moment, you will never see again. So it is with the misery that has challenged your life: Let it go, let it pass away. The brilliance of morning is in sharp contrast to the darkness of night; simply stated, it was night, but now it is day. Perhaps David understood the aftereffects of traumatic deliverance when he said, "Weeping may endure for a night, but joy cometh in the morning" (Ps. 30:5b).

There is such a security that comes when we are safe in the arms of God. It is when we become secure in our relationship with God that we begin to allow the past to fall from us as a garment. We remember it, but choose not to wear it! I am convinced that resting in the relationship that we have with God heals us from the feelings of vulnerability. It is a shame that many Christians have not yet rested in the promise of God. Everyone needs reassurance. Little girls as well as grown women need that sense of security. In the process of creating Eve, the mother of all living, His timing was crucial. In fact, God did not unveil her until everything she needed was provided. From establishment to relationship, all things were in order. Innately the woman tends to need stability. She wants no sudden changes that disrupt or compromise her security.

She was meant to be covered and originally Adam was her covering, to nurture and protect her. My sister, you were made to be covered even as a child. If someone "uncovered" you, there is a feeling of being violated. Even when these feelings are suppressed, and they often are, they are still powerful. I think it is interesting that when the Bible talks about incest, it uses the word *uncover*. Sexual abuse violates the covering of the family and the responsible persons whom we looked to for guidance.

This stripping away of right relation leaves us exposed to the infinite reality of corrupt, lustful imaginations. Like fruit peeled too soon, it is damaging to uncover what God had wanted to remain protected! Who among us can repeel a banana once it has been peeled? The Bible says, "With men it is impossible, but not with God: for with God all things are possible" (Mk. 10:27).

> *None of you shall approach to any that is near*
> *of kin to him, to uncover their nakedness: I am*
> *the Lord.* Leviticus 18:6

To molest a child is to uncover them. It leaves them feeling unprotected. Do you realize that one of the things the blood of Jesus Christ does is cover us? Like Noah's sons who covered their father's nakedness, the blood of Jesus will cover the uncovered. He will not allow you to spend the rest of your life exposed and violated. In Ezekiel, He speaks a message to the nation of Israel with an illustration of an abused woman. He speaks about how, as a child, this little girl was not cared for properly. But the Lord passed by her and salted, swaddled and cared for her as a baby. He says the baby would have bled to death if He hadn't stopped the bleeding. Did you know that God can stop the bleeding of an abused child? Even as you grow older, He still watches out for you! He will cover your nakedness.

> *Then I passed by and saw you kicking about in*
> *your blood, and as you lay there in your blood*
> *I said to you, "Live!" I made you grow like a*
> *plant of the field. You grew up and developed*
> *and became the most beautiful of jewels. Your*

*breasts were formed and your hair grew, you
who were naked and bare. Later I passed by,
and when I looked at you and saw that you
were old enough for love, I spread the corner
of my garment over you and covered your
nakedness. I gave you My solemn oath and
entered into a covenant with you, declares the
Sovereign Lord, and you became Mine. I
bathed you with water and washed the blood
from you and put ointments on you. I clothed
you with an embroidered dress and put leather
sandals on you. I dressed you in fine linen and
covered you with costly garments.*
Ezekiel 16:6-10 (NIV)

Reach out and embrace the fact that God has been
watching over you all of your life. My sister, He covers
you, He clothes you, and He blesses you! Rejoice in Him
in spite of the broken places. God's grace is sufficient for
your needs and your scars. He will anoint you with oil.
The anointing of the Lord be upon you now! May it bathe,
heal and strengthen you as never before.

For the hurting, God has intensive care. There will be
a time in your life when God nurtures you through crisis
situations. You may not even realize how many times God
has intervened to relieve the tensions and stresses of day-
to-day living. Every now and then He does us a favor. Yes,
a favor, something we didn't earn or can't even explain,
except as the loving hand of God. He knows when the
load is overwhelming. Many times He moves (it seems to
us) just in the knick of time.

The Bible instructs the men to dwell with women according to knowledge (1 Pet. 3:7). It will pay every husband to understand that many, many women do not deal easily with such stress as unpaid bills and financial disorder. A feeling of security is a plus, especially in reference to the home. That same principle is important when it comes to your relationship with God. He is constantly reassuring us that we might have a consolation and a hope for the soul, the mind and emotions, steadfast and unmovable. He gives us security and assurance.

> *Because God wanted to make the unchanging nature of His purpose very clear to the heirs of what was promised, He confirmed it with an oath. God did this so that, by two unchangeable things in which it is impossible for God to lie, we who have fled to take hold of the hope offered to us may be greatly encouraged.*
> Hebrews 6:17-18 (NIV)

"Also thou shalt lie down, and none shall make thee afraid" (Job 11:19a), is the word of God to you. God wants to bring you to a place of rest, where there is no pacing the floor, no glaring at those with whom you are involved, through frightened eyes. Like a frightened animal backed into a corner, we can become fearful and angry because we don't feel safe. Christ says, "Woman, thou art loosed!"

There is no torment like inner torment. How can you run from yourself? No matter what you achieve in life, if the clanging, rattling chains of old ghosts are not laid to rest, you will not have any real sense of peace and inner joy. God says, "None shall make thee afraid." A perfect love casts out fear (1 Jn. 4:18)! It is a miserable feeling to spend your life in fear. Many grown women live in a fear that resulted from broken arrow experiences. This kind of fear can manifest itself in jealousy, depression and many other distresses. As you allow the past to pass over you as waters moving in the sea, you will begin to live and rest in a new assurance. God loves you so much that He is even concerned about your rest. Take authority over every flashback and every dream that keeps you linked to the past. Even as we share together here, the peace of God will do a new thing in your life. I encourage you to claim Job 11:16-19 as yours.

I was raised in the rich, robust Appalachian mountains of West Virginia where the plush greenery accentuates the majestic peaks of the rugged mountainous terrain. The hills sit around the river's edge like court stenographers, recording the events of the ages without expression or interference. I learned as a child how to entertain myself by running up and down the trails and scenic paths of our community, splashing in the creek beds and singing songs to the wind. This kind of simplistic joy is, to me, characteristic of that time when children were not as complex as they are now.

If you know much about the Appalachian mountains, you know they were the backyard for many, many Indians in days gone by. There are many large, man-made hills, which the Indians called mounds, that served as cemeteries for the more affluent members of the tribes. During my childhood, occasionally either my classmates or myself would find old Indian memorabilia in the rocks and creek beds in the hills. The most common thing to find would be discarded arrowheads carved to a point and beaten flat. Perhaps an Indian brave from the pages of history had thrown away the arrow, assuming he had gotten out of it all the possible use he could. Though worthless to him, it was priceless to us as we retrieved it from its hiding place and saved it in a safe and sacred place. I believe that God gathers discarded children who, like arrows, have been thrown away from the quiver of vain and ruthless people. If children are like arrows in the quiver of a mighty man, then broken arrows who are thrown away by that man belong to God, who is forever finding treasure in the discarded refuse of our confused society.

And they shall be Mine, saith the Lord of hosts,
in that day when I make up My jewels; and I
will spare them, as a man spareth his own son
that serveth him. Malachi 3:17

Please, Holy Spirit, translate these meager words into a deluge of cleansing and renewal. I pray that you who have been marred, would allow the reconstructive hand of the Potter to mend the broken places in your lives. Amidst affairs and struggles, needs and incidents, may the peace and calmness of knowing God cause the birth of fresh dreams. But most of all, may it lay to rest old fears.

Chapter 3

THAT WAS THEN

Many Christians experienced the new birth early in their childhood. It is beneficial to have the advantage of Christian ethics. I'm not sure what it would have been like to have been raised in the church and been insulated from worldliness and sin. Sometimes I envy those who have been able to live victoriously all of their lives. Most of us have not had that kind of life. My concern is the many persons who have lost their sensitivity for others and who suffer from spiritual arrogance. Jesus condemned the Pharisees for their spiritual arrogance, yet many times that self-righteous spirit creeps into the Church.

There are those who define holiness as what one wears or what a person eats. For years churches displayed the name "holiness" because they monitored a person's outward appearance. They weren't truly looking at character. Often they were carried away with whether someone should wear makeup or jewelry when thousands of people were destroying themselves on drugs and prostitution. Priorities were confused. Unchurched people who came to church had no idea why the minister would emphasize outward apparel when people were bleeding inside.

The fact is, we were all born in sin and shaped in iniquity. We have no true badge of righteousness that we can wear on the outside. God concluded all are in sin so He might save us from ourselves (Gal. 3:22). It wasn't the act of sin, but the state of sin, that brought us into condemnation. We were born in sin, equally and individually shaped in iniquity, and not one race or sociological group has escaped the fact that we are Adam's sinful heritage.

No one person needs any more of the blood of Jesus than the other. Jesus died once and for all. Humanity must come to God on equal terms, each individual totally helpless to earn his or her way to Him. When we come to Him with this attitude, He raises us up by the blood of Christ. He doesn't raise us up because we do good things. He raises us up because we have faith in the finished work on the cross.

Many in the Church were striving for holiness. What we were striving to perfect had already fallen and will only be restored at the second coming of the Lord. We were trying to perfect flesh. Flesh is in enmity against God, whether we paint it or not.

The Church frequently has, and still does, major on the minors. When that begins to happen, it is a sign that the Church has lost touch with the world and with the inspiration of the Lord. It is no longer reaching out to the lost. A church that focuses on the external has lost its passion for souls. When we come into that position, we have attained a pseudo-holiness. It's a false sanctity.

What is holiness? To understand it, we must first separate the pseudo from the genuine because, when you come into a church, it is possible to walk away feeling like a second-class citizen. Many start going overboard trying to be a super spiritual person in order to compensate for an embarrassing past. You can't earn deliverance. You have to just receive it by faith. Christ is the only righteousness that God will accept. If outward sanctity had impressed God, Christ would have endorsed the Pharisees.

However, there is a sanctity of your spirit that comes through the blood of the Lord Jesus Christ and sanctifies the innermost part of your being. Certainly, once you get cleaned up in your spirit, it will be reflected in your character and conduct. You won't be like Mary the mother of Jesus and dress like Mary Magdalene did before she met the Master. The Spirit of the Lord will give you boundaries. On the other hand, people must be loosed from the chains of guilt and condemnation. Many women in particular have been bound by manipulative messages that specialize in control and dominance.

The Church must open its doors and allow people who have a past to enter in. What often happens is they're spending years in the back pew trying to pay through obeisance for something in the past. Congregations often are unwilling to release reformed women. Remember, the same blood that cleanses the man can restore the woman also.

The Bible never camouflaged the weaknesses of the people God used. God used David. God used Abraham. We must divorce our embarrassment about wounded people. Yes, we've got wounded people. Yes, we've got hurting people. Sometimes they break the boundaries and they become lascivious and out of control and we have to readmit them into the hospital and allow them to be treated again. That's what the Church is designed to do. The Church is a hospital for wounded souls.

The staff in a hospital understand that periodically people get sick and they need a place to recover. Now, I'm not condoning the sin. I'm just explaining that it's a reality. Many of those in Scripture were unholy. The only holy man out of all of the characters in the Bible is Jesus Christ, the righteousness of God.

We have all wrestled with something, though it may not always be the same challenge. My struggle may not be yours. If I'm wrestling with something that's not a problem to you, you do not have the responsibility for judging me when all the while you are wrestling with something equally as incriminating.

Jesus' actions were massively different from ours. He focused on hurting people. Every time He saw a hurting person, He reached out and ministered to their need. Once when He was preaching, He looked through the crowd and saw a man with a withered hand. He immediately healed him (Mk. 3:1-5). He sat with the prostitutes and the winebibbers, not the upper echelon of His community. Jesus surrounded Himself with broken, bleeding, dirty people. He called a woman who was crippled and bent over (Lk. 13:11-13). She had come to church and sat in the synagogue for years and years and nobody had helped that woman until Jesus saw her. He called her to the forefront.

At first when I thought about His calling her, I thought, "How rude to call her." Why didn't He speak the word and heal her in her seat? Perhaps God wants to see us moving toward Him. We need to invest in our own deliverance. We will bring a testimony out of a test. I also believe that someone else there had problems. When we can see someone else overcoming a handicap, it helps us to overcome.

We can't know how long it took her to get up to the front. Handicapped people don't move as fast as others do. As believers, we often don't grow as fast as other people grow because we've been suffering for a long time. We are incapacitated. Often what is simple for one person is extremely difficult for another. Jesus challenged this woman's limitations. He called her anyway.

Thank God He calls women with a past. He reaches out and says, "Get up! You can come to Me." Regardless of what a person has done, or what kind of abuse one has suffered, He still calls. We may think our secret is worse than anyone else's. Rest assured that He knows all about it, and still draws us with an immutable call.

Jesus said, "Come unto Me, all ye that labour and are heavy laden, and I will give you rest" (Mt. 11:28).

No matter how difficult life seems, people with a past need to make their way to Jesus. Regardless of the obstacles within and without, they must reach Him. You may have a baby out of wedlock cradled in your arms, but keep pressing on. You may have been abused and molested and never able to talk to anyone about it, but don't cease reaching out for Him. You don't have to tell everyone your entire history. Just know that He calls, on purpose, women with a past. He knows your history, but He called you anyway.

God will give you a miracle. He'll do it powerfully and publicly. Many will say, "Is this the same woman that was bent over and wounded in the church?" Perhaps some will think, "Is this the same woman who had one foot in the church and the other in an affair?"

Many of the people who were a part of the ministry of Jesus' earthly life were people with colorful pasts. Some had indeed always looked for the Messiah to come. Others were involved in things that were immoral and inappropriate.

A good example is Matthew. He was a man who worked in an extremely distasteful profession. He was a tax collector. Few people like tax collectors still today. Their reputation was even worse at that time in history. Matthew collected taxes for the Roman empire. He had to have been considered a traitor by those who were faithful

Jews. Romans were their oppressors. How could he have forsaken his heritage and joined the Romans?

Tax collectors did more than simply receive taxes for the benefit of the government. They were frequently little better than common extortioners. They had to collect a certain amount for Rome, but anything they could collect above that set figure was considered the collector's commission. Therefore they frequently claimed excessive taxes. Often they acted like common thieves.

Regardless of his past, Jesus called Matthew to be a disciple. Later he served as a great apostle and wrote one of the books of the New Testament. Much of the history and greatness of Jesus would be lost to us were it not for Jesus calling Matthew, a man with a past. We must maintain a strong line of demarcation between a person's past and present.

These were the people Jesus wanted to reach. He was criticized for being around questionable characters. Everywhere He went the oppressed and the rejected followed Him. They knew that He offered mercy and forgiveness.

And it came to pass, as Jesus sat at meat in the house, behold, many publicans and sinners came and sat down with Him and His disciples. And when the Pharisees saw it, they said unto His disciples, Why eateth your Master with publicans and sinners? But when Jesus heard that, He said unto them, They that be whole need not a physician, but they that are sick. Matthew 9:10-12

People with a past have always been able to come to Jesus. He makes them into something wonderful and marvelous. It is said that Mary Magdalene was a prostitute. Christ was moved with compassion for even this base kind of human existence. He never used a prostitute for sex, but He certainly loved them into the Kingdom of God.

When Christ was teaching in the temple courts, there were those who tried to trap Him in His words. They knew that His ministry appealed to the masses of lowly people. They thought that if they could get Him to say some condemning things, the people wouldn't follow Him anymore.

And the scribes and Pharisees brought unto Him a woman taken in adultery; and when they had set her in the midst, they said unto Him, Master, this woman was taken in adultery, in the very act. Now Moses in the law commanded us, that such should be stoned: but what sayest thou? This they said, tempting Him, that they might have to accuse Him. But Jesus stooped down, and with His finger wrote on the ground, as though He heard them not. So when they continued asking Him, He lifted up Himself, and said unto them, He that is without sin among you, let him first cast a stone at her. John 8:3-7

Clearly Jesus saw the foolish religious pride in their hearts. He was not condoning the sin of adultery. He simply understood the need to meet people where they were and minister to their need. He saw the pride in the Pharisees and ministered correction to that pride. He saw the wounded woman and ministered forgiveness. Justice demanded that she be stoned to death. Mercy threw the case out of court.

Have you ever wondered where the man was who had been committing adultery with this woman? She had been caught in the very act. Surely they knew who the man was. There still seems to be a double standard today when it comes to sexual sin. Often we look down on a woman because of her past but overlook who she is now. Jesus, however, knew the power of a second chance.

When Jesus had lifted up Himself, and saw none but the woman, He said unto her, Woman, where are those thine accusers? hath no man condemned thee? She said, No man, Lord. And Jesus said unto her, Neither do I condemn thee: go, and sin no more.
John 8:10-11

There are those today who are very much like this woman. They have come into the Church. Perhaps they have made strong commitments to Christ and have the very Spirit of God living within them. Yet they walk as cripples. They have been stoned and ridiculed. They may not be physically broken and bowed over, but they are wounded within. Somehow the Church must find room to throw off condemnation and give life and healing.

43

The blood of Jesus is efficacious, cleansing the woman who feels unclean. How can we reject what He has cleansed and made whole? Just as He said to the woman then, He proclaims today, "Neither do I condemn thee: go and sin no more." How can the Church do any less?

The chains that bind are often from events that we have no control over. The woman who is abused is not responsible for the horrible events that happened in her past. Other times the chains are there because we have willfully lived lives that bring bondage and pain. Regardless of the source, Jesus comes to set us free. He is unleashing the women of His Church. He forgives, heals and restores. Women can find the potential of their future because of His wonderful power operating in their lives.

*C*hapter 4

The Victim Survives

I would like to share what is perhaps one of the most powerful stories in the Bible. It takes place in ancient Israel. The chosen people had become a great empire. Israel was at its zenith under the leadership of a godly king named David. There can be no argument that David frequently allowed his passions to lead him into moral failure. However, he was a man who recognized his failures and repented. He was a man who sought God's heart.

Although David longed to follow God, some of his passions and lust were inherited by his children. Maybe they learned negative things from their father's failures. That is a tendency we must resist. We ought not repeat the failure of our fathers. We are most vulnerable, however, to our father's weaknesses.

And it came to pass after this, that Absalom the son of David had a fair sister, whose name was

Tamar; and Amnon the son of David loved her. And Amnon was so vexed, that he fell sick for his sister Tamar; for she was a virgin; and Amnon thought it hard for him to do anything to her. But Amnon had a friend, whose name was Jonadab, the son of Shimeah, David's brother: and Jonadab was a very subtle man. And he said unto him, Why art thou, being the king's son, lean from day to day? wilt thou not tell me? And Amnon said unto him, I love Tamar, my brother Absalom's sister. And Jonadab said unto him, Lay thee down on thy bed, and make thyself sick: and when thy father cometh to see thee, say unto him, I pray thee, let my sister Tamar come, and give me meat, and dress the meat in my sight, that I may see it, and eat it at her hand. So Amnon lay down, and made himself sick: and when the king was come to see him, Amnon said unto the king, I pray thee, let Tamar my sister come, and make me a couple of cakes in my sight, that I may eat at her hand. Then David sent home to Tamar saying, Go now to thy brother Amnon's house, and dress him meat. So Tamar went to her brother Amnon's house; and he was laid down. And she took flour, and kneaded it, and made cakes in his sight, and did bake the cakes. And she took a pan, and poured them out before him; but he refused to eat. And Amnon said, Have out all men from me. And they went out every man from him. And Amnon said unto Tamar, Bring the meat into the chamber, that I may eat of thine hand. And Tamar took the cakes which she had made, and brought them into the chamber to Amnon her brother. And when she had brought them unto him to eat, he took hold of her, and said unto her, Come lie with me, my sister. And she answered him, Nay, my brother, do not force me; for no such thing ought to be done in Israel: do not thou this folly. And I, whither shall I cause my shame to go? and as for thee, thou shalt be as one of the fools in Israel. Now therefore, I pray thee, speak unto the king; for he will not withhold me from thee. Howbeit he would not hearken unto her voice: but, being stronger than she, forced her, and lay with her. Then Amnon hated her exceedingly; so that the hatred wherewith he hated her was greater than the love wherewith he had loved her. And Amnon said unto her, Arise, be gone. And she said unto him, There is no cause: this evil in sending me away is greater than the other that thou didst unto me. But he would not hearken unto her. Then he called his servant that ministered unto him, and said, Put now this woman out from me, and bolt the door after her. And she had a garment of divers colours upon her: for with such robes were the king's daughters that were virgins apparelled. Then his servant brought her out, and bolted the door after her. And Tamar put ashes on her head, and rent her garment of divers colours that was on her, and laid her hand on her head, and went on crying.

*And Absalom her brother said unto her, Hath
Amnon thy brother been with thee? but hold
now thy peace, my sister: he is thy brother;
regard not this thing. So Tamar remained deso-
late in her brother Absalom's house. But when
king David heard of all these things, he was
very wroth.* 2 Samuel 13:1-21

The name *Tamar* means "palm tree." Tamar is a survivor. She stands in summer and spring. She even faces
fall with leaves when other trees lose theirs. She still
stands. When the cold blight of winter stands up in her
face, she withstands the chilly winds and remains green
throughout the winter. Tamar is a survivor. You are a survivor. Through hard times God has granted you the tenacity to endure stresses and strains.

It's hard for me as a man to fully understand how
horrible rape is for women. I can sympathize, but the vio-
lation is incomprehensible. I don't feel as vulnerable to
being raped as a woman would. However, I have come to
realize that rape is another creature inflicting his will on
someone without her permission. It is more than just the
act of sex. It is someone victimizing you. There are all
kinds of rape—emotional, spiritual and physical. There
are many ways to be victimized. Abuse is abnormal use.
It is terrible to misuse or abuse anyone.

Many women feel guilty about things they had no
control over. They feel guilty about being victimized.
Often their original intention was to help another, but in
the process they are damaged. Tamar was the king's
daughter. She was a virgin. She was a "good girl." She

didn't do anything immoral. It is amazing that her own brother would be so filled with desire that he would go to such lengths to destroy his sister. He thought he was in love. It wasn't love. It was lust. He craved her so intensely that he lost his appetite for food. He was visibly distorted with passion. Love is a giving force, while lust is a selfish compulsion centralized on gratification.

It is frightening to think about the nights that he plotted and conjured her destruction. The intensity of his passion for her was awesome. So much so, that even his father and cousin recognized that something had altered his behavior. He was filled with lustful passion for her.

Amnon draws a picture for us of how badly the enemy wants to violate God's children. He is planning and plotting your destruction. He has watched you with wanton eyes. He has great passion and perseverance. Jesus told Peter, "Satan hath desired to have you, that he may sift you as wheat: but I have prayed for thee..." (Lk. 22:31-32). Satan lusts after God's children. He wants you. He craves for you with an animalistic passion. He awaits an opportunity for attack. In addition, he loves to use people to fulfill the same kinds of lust upon one another.

Desire is a motivating force. It can make you do things you never thought yourself capable of doing. Lust can make a man break his commitment to himself. It will cause people to reach after things they never thought they would reach for.

Like Peter, you may have gone through some horrible times, but Jesus intercedes on your behalf. No matter the struggles women have faced, confidence is found in the ministry of our High Priest. He prays for you. Faith comes when you recognize that you can't help yourself. Only trust in Christ can bring you through. Many have suffered mightily, but Christ gives the strength to overcome the attacks of satan and human, selfish lust.

Often the residual effects of being abused linger for many years. Some never find deliverance because they never allow Christ to come into the dark places of their life. Jesus has promised to set you free from every curse of the past. If you have suffered abuse, please know that He will bring you complete healing. He wants the whole person well—in body, emotions and spirit. He will deliver you from all the residue of your past. Perhaps the incident is over but the crippling is still there. He also will deal with the crippling that's left in your life.

One of the things that makes many women particularly vulnerable to different types of abuse and manipulation is their maternal instinct. Wicked men frequently capitalize on this tendency in order to have their way with women. Mothers like to take care of little helpless babies. It seems that the more helpless a man acts, the more maternal you become. Women instinctively are nurturers, reaching out to needy people in order to nurture, love and provide inner strength. All too often, these healthy desires are taken advantage of by those who would fulfill their own lusts. The gift of discernment must operate in your life. There are many wonderful men. But I must warn you against Amnon. He is dangerous.

The number of cases of violence within relationships and marriages is growing at an alarming rate. The incidence of date rape is reaching epidemic proportions. The fastest growing form of murder today is within relationships. Husbands and wives and girlfriends and boyfriends are killing one another. Often women have taken to murder in order to escape the constant violence of an abusive husband. It is important that you do not allow loneliness to coerce you into Amnon's bed.

Another form of abuse is more subtle. There are those men who often coerce women into a sexual relationship by claiming that they love them. Deception is emotional rape! It is a terrible feeling to be used by someone. Looking for love in all the wrong places leads to a feeling of abuse. A deceiver may continually promise that he will leave his wife for his lover. This woman holds on to that hope, but it never seems to come true. He makes every kind of excuse possible for taking advantage of her, and she, because of her vulnerability, follows blindly along until the relationship has gone so far that she is trapped.

Men who have sex with women without being committed to them are just as guilty of abuse as a rapist. A woman may have given her body to such a man, but she did so because of certain expectations. When someone uses another person for sex by misleading them, it is the same as physical rape. The abuse is more subtle, but it amounts to the same thing. Both the abuser and the victim are riding into a blazing inferno. Anything can happen when a victim has had enough.

Some women suffer from low self-esteem. They are victims and they don't even know it. Perhaps every time something goes wrong, you think it's your fault. It is not your fault if you are being abused in this way; it is your fault if you don't allow God's Word to arrest sin and weakness in your life. It is time to let go of every ungodly relationship. Do it now!

When Tamar came into that ancient Israeli bedroom, her brother took advantage of her maternal instincts. He told her that he needed help. He sought her sympathy. Once she gave in to his requests for help, he violently raped her. Although the circumstances may be different, the same thing is happening today.

The kind of violent act that Amnon performed that night was more than an offense against a young lady. He offended God and society by committing incest. There are those who attend church who are incestuous. It still happens today, but God is saying that enough is enough!

Some have been abused, misused and victimized. Some played a part in their own demise. There are those who live in fear and pain because of the immoral relationships that took place in the home. If you know this kind of pain, the Lord wants to heal you. Those who have a desperate need for male attention, have usually come from a situation where there has been an absence of positive male role models in the home. Perhaps you didn't get enough nurturing as a girl. Therefore, it becomes easy to compromise and do anything to find male acceptance and love.

The Lord is calling the hurting to Him. He will fill that void in your life. He wants to be that heavenly Father who will mend your heart with a positive role model. Through the Spirit, He wants to hold and nurture you. Millions have longed for a positive hug and nurturing embrace from fathers without ever receiving what they longed for. There is a way to fill that emptiness inside. It is through a relationship with God.

Men, God is healing us so we can recognize that a woman who is not our wife is to be treated as our sister. Women must learn that they can have a platonic relationship with men. A brotherly and sisterly love does not include sexual intimacy. It does not include self-gratification.

There is a place in the heart of most women for an intimate and yet platonic relationship. Big brothers tend to protect their little sisters. They tend to watch for traps that may be placed in the sisters' way. Abused women have confused ideas abut relationships, and may not understand a healthy platonic relationship with the opposite sex. This confusion comes from the past. One lady said that she could never trust a man who didn't sleep with her. Actually, she had a long history of victimization that led to her poor view of relationships.

Society often places a woman's worth on her sexual appeal. Nothing is further from the truth. Self-esteem cannot be earned by performance in bed. Society suggests that the only thing men want is sex. Although the male sex drive is very strong, all men are not like Amnon. Men, in general, are not the enemy. We cannot use Amnon as a

basis to evaluate all men. Do not allow an Amnon experience to taint your future. Draw a line of demarcation and
say to yourself, "That was then and this is now!"

The Song of Solomon shows a progression of the
relationship between the author and his wife. First she
was his sister, then she became his bride. He also wrote of
protecting a little sister. There are many new converts in
the Church who are to be treated as little sisters. Solomon
says, " enclose her with boards of cedar" (Song. 8:9). The
Church is God's cedar chest!

God's people are to nurture and protect one another.
It makes no difference how tempestuous our past life has
been. Even in the face of abuse, God still cares. Allow
Him the privilege of doing what Absalom did for Tamar.
He took her in. "He that dwelleth in the secret place of
the most High shall abide under the shadow of the
Almighty" (Ps. 91:1). Tamar lay outside Amnon's door—
a fragmented, bruised rose petal. Her dreams were shat-
tered. Her confidence was violated. Her virginity was
desecrated. But Absalom took her into his domain. Did
you know that God has intensive care? He will take you
in His arms. That love of God is flowing into broken lives
all over the country. Don't believe for one moment that no
one cares; God cares and the Church is learning to become
a conduit of that concern. At last, we are in the school of
love. Jesus said, "By this shall all men know that ye are
My disciples, if ye have love one to another" (Jn. 13:35).

Love embraces the totality of the other person. It is
impossible to completely and effectively love someone
without being included in that other person's history. Our

history has made us who we are. The images, scars and victories that we live with have shaped us into the people we have become. We will never know who a person is until we understand where they have been.

The secret of being transformed from a vulnerable victim to a victorious, loving person is found in the ability to open your past to someone responsible enough to share your weaknesses and pains. "Bear ye one another's burdens, and so fulfill the law of Christ" (Gal. 6:2). You don't have to keep reliving it. You can release it.

There can be no better first step toward deliverance than to find a Christian counselor or pastor and come out of hiding. Of course, some care should be taken. No one is expected to air their personal life to everyone or even everywhere. However, if you seek God's guidance and the help of confident leadership, you will find someone who can help you work through the pain and suffering of being a victim. The Church is a body. No one operates independent of another. We are all in this walk together, and therefore can build one another up and carry some of the load with which our sisters are burdened.

Tamar was victimized brutally, yet she survived. There is hope for victims. There is no need to feel weak when one has Jesus Christ. His power is enough to bring about the kinds of changes that will set you free. He is calling, through the work of the Holy Spirit, for you to be set free.

Chapter 5

WALK INTO THE NEWNESS

Amnon was wicked. He brutally raped his sister Tamar. He destroyed her destiny and her future. He slashed her self-esteem. He spoiled her integrity. He broke her femininity like a twig under his feet. He assassinated her character. She went into his room a virgin with a future. When it was over, she was a bleeding, trembling, crying mass of pain.

That is one of the saddest stories in the Bible. It also reveals what people can do to one another if left alone without God. For when Amnon and Tamar were left alone, he assassinated her. The body survived, but her femininity was destroyed. She felt as though she would never be the woman that she would have been had it not happened.

Have you ever had anything happen to you that changed you forever? Somehow, you were like a palm tree and you survived. Yet you knew you would never be the same. Perhaps you have spent every day since then bowed over. You could in no wise lift up yourself. You shout. You sing. You skip. But when no one is looking, when the crowd is gone and the lights are out, you are still that trembling, crying, bleeding mass of pain that is abused, bowed, bent backward, and crippled.

Maybe you are in the Church, but you are in trouble. People move all around you, and you laugh, even entertain them. You are fun to be around. But they don't know. You can't seem to talk about what happened in your life.

The Bible says Tamar was in trouble. The worst part about it is, after Amnon had abused her, he didn't even want her. He had messed up her life and spoiled what she was proud of. He assassinated her future and damaged her prospects. He destroyed her integrity and self-esteem. He had changed her countenance forever. Afterward, he did not even want her. Tamar said, "What you're doing to me now is worse than what you did to me at first." She said, "Raping me was horrible, but not wanting me is worse" (2 Sam. 13:16). When women feel unwanted, it destroys their sense of esteem and value.

Some of you have gone through divorces, tragedies and adulterous relationships, and you've been left feeling unwanted. You can't shout over that sort of thing. You can't leap over that kind of wall. It injures something about you that changes how you relate to everyone else for the rest of your life. Amnon didn't even want Tamar afterwards. She pleaded with him, "Don't throw me away." She was fighting for the last strands of her femininity. Amnon called a servant and said, "Throw her out."

The Bible says he hated her with a greater intensity than with which he had loved her before (2 Sam. 13:15).

God knows that the Amnon in your life really does not love you. He's out to abuse you. The servant picked Tamar up, opened the door and threw that victimized woman out. She lay on the ground outside the door with nowhere to go. He told the servant, "Lock the door."

What do you do when you are trapped in a transitory state, neither in nor out? You're left lying at the door, torn up and disturbed, trembling and intimidated. The Bible says she cried. What do you do when you don't know what to do? Filled with regrets, pains, nightmare experiences, seemingly unable to find relief... unable to rise above it, she stayed on the ground. She cried.

She had a coat, a cape of many colors. It was a sign of her virginity and of her future. She was going to give it to her husband one day. She sat there and ripped it up. She was saying, "I have no future. It wasn't just that he took my body. He took my future. He took my esteem and value away."

Many of you have been physically or emotionally raped and robbed. You survived, but you left a substantial degree of self-esteem in Amnon's bed. Have you lost the road map that directs you back to where you were before?

There's a call out in the Spirit for hurting women. The Lord says, "I want you." No matter how many men like Amnon have told you, "I don't want you," God says, "I want you. I've seen you bent over. I've seen the aftereffects of what happened to you. I've seen you at your worst moment. I still want you." God has not changed His mind. God loves with an everlasting love.

When Jesus encountered the infirm woman of Luke 13, He called out to her. There may have been many fine women present that day, but the Lord didn't call them forward. He reached around all of them and found that crippled woman in the back. He called forth the wounded, hurting woman with a past. He issued the Spirit's call to those who had their value and self-esteem destroyed by the intrusion of vicious circumstances.

The infirm woman must have thought, "He wants me. He wants *me*. I'm frayed and torn, but He wants me. I have been through trouble. I have been through this trauma, but He wants me." Perhaps she thought no one would ever want her again, but Jesus wanted her. He had a plan.

She may have known that it would take a while for her life to be completely put back together. She had many things to overcome. She was handicapped. She was probably filled with insecurities. Yet Jesus still called her forth for His touch.

If you can identify with the feelings of this infirm woman, then know that He's waiting on you and that He wants you. He sees your struggling and He knows all about your pain. He knows what happened to you 18 years ago or 10 years ago or even last week. With patience He waits for you, as the father waited for the prodigal son. Jesus says to the hurting and crippled, "I want you enough to wait for you to hobble your way back home."

Now God says, "I'm going to deliver you and heal you. Now I'm going to renew you and release you. I'm going to tell you who you really are. Now I'm ready to reveal to you why you had to go through what you did to become what you shall become." He says, "Now I'm going to tell you a secret, something between you and I no one else knows. Amnon didn't know. Your boyfriend didn't know, your first husband didn't know. I'll tell you something that your father, uncle, brother or whoever abused you had no knowledge of. Just realize that you are the daughter of a king. Your Father is the King."

When the infirmed woman came to Jesus, He proclaimed her freedom. Now she stands erect for the first time in 18 years. When you come to Jesus, He will cause you to stand in His strength. You will know how important you are to Him. Part of your recovery is to learn how to stand up and live in the "now" of life instead of the "then" of yesterday. That was then but this is now.

I proclaim to the abused: There is a healing going into your spirit right now. I speak life to you. I speak deliverance to you. I speak restoration to you. All in the mighty name of Jesus, in the invincible, all-powerful, everlasting name of Jesus. I proclaim victory to you. You will recover the loss you suffered at the hands of your abuser. You will get back every stolen item. He will heal that broken twig. He will rebuild your self-esteem, your self-respect, and your integrity.

All you need do is allow His power and anointing to touch the hurting places. He will take care of the secrets. He touches the places where you've been assassinated. He knows the woman you would have been, the woman you should have been, the woman you could have been. God is healing and restoring her in you as you call out to Him.

The enemy wanted to change your destiny through a series of events, but God will restore you to wholeness as if the events had never happened. The triumphant woman locked inside shall come forth to where she belongs. He's delivering her. He's releasing her. He's restoring her. He's building her back. He's bringing her out. He's delivering by the power of His Spirit. "Not by might, nor by power, but by My spirit, saith the Lord of hosts" (Zech. 4:6).

The anointing of the living God is reaching out to you. He calls you forth to set you free. When you reach out to Him and allow the Holy Spirit to have His way, His anointing is present to deliver you. Demons will tremble. He wants to keep you at the door, but never let you enter. He wants to keep you down. Now his power is broken in your life.

Tamar knew the feeling of desertion. She understood that she was cast out. However, the Bible explains that Absalom came and said, "I'm going to take you in." You too may have been lying at the door. Perhaps you didn't have anywhere to go. You may have been half in and half out. You were broken and demented and disturbed. But God sent Absalom to restore his sister.

In this instance, Absalom depicts the purpose of real ministry. Thank God for the Church. It's the place where you can come broken and disgusted, and be healed, delivered and set free in the name of Jesus.

Jesus said, "The Spirit of the Lord is upon Me, because He hath anointed Me to preach the gospel to the poor; He hath sent Me to heal the brokenhearted, to preach deliverance to the captives, and recovering of sight to the blind, to set at liberty them that are bruised" (Lk. 4:18).

You may have thought that you would never rejoice again. God declares that you can have freedom in Him— now! The joy that He brings can be restored to your soul. He identifies with your pain and suffering. He knows what it is like to suffer abuse at the hands of others. Yet He proclaims joy and strength. He will give you the garment of praise instead of the spirit of heaviness (Is. 61:3).

Once you have called out to Him, you can lift up your hands in praise. No matter what you have suffered, you can hold up your head. Regardless of who has hurt you, hold up your head! Forget how many times you've been married. Put aside those who mistreated you. You may have been a lesbian. You may have been a crack addict. It doesn't matter who you were. You may have even been molested. You can't change where you have been, but you can change where you are going.

Lift up your heads, O ye gates; even lift them up, ye everlasting doors; and the King of glory shall come in. Who is this King of glory? The

Lord of hosts, He is the King of glory. Selah.
Psalm 24:9-10

He will restore to you that which the cankerworm and the locust ate up (Joel 2:25). He said, "I'm going to give it back to you." Maybe you wrestle with guilt. You've been hearing babies crying in your spirit. You feel so dirty. You've had abortions. You've been misused and abused. The devil keeps bringing up to you your failures of the past.

Come now, and let us reason together, saith the
Lord: though your sins be as scarlet, they shall
be as white as snow; though they be red like
crimson, they shall be as wool. Isaiah 1:18

All my life I have had a tremendous compassion for hurting people. When other people would put their foot on them, I always tended to have a ministry of mercy. Perhaps it is because I've had my own pain. When you have suffered, it makes you able to relate to other people's pain. The Lord settled me in a ministry that just tends to cater to hurting people. Sometimes when I minister, I find myself fighting back tears. Sometimes I can hear the cries of anguished people in the crowd.

Like Tamar, you're a survivor. You should celebrate your survival. Instead of agonizing over your tragedies, you should celebrate your victory and thank God you made it. I charge you to step over your adversity and walk into the newness. It is like stepping from a storm into the sunshine. Just step into it now.

God has blessed me with two little boys and two little daughters. As a father, I have found that I have a ministry of hugs. When something happens, and I really can't fix it, I just hug them. I can't change how other people treated them. I can't change what happened at school. I can't make the teacher like them. I can't take away the insults. But I can hug them!

I believe the best nurses are the ones who have been patients. They have compassion on the victim. If anyone understands the plight of women, it ought to be women. The Church needs to develop a ministry of hugs. The touch of the Master sets us free. The touch of a fellow pilgrim lets us know we are not alone in our plight.

The Holy Spirit is calling for the broken, infirm women to come to Jesus. He will restore and deliver. How do we come to Jesus? We come to His Body, the Church. It is in the Church that we can hear the Word of God. The Church gives us strength and nourishment. The Church is to be the place where we share our burdens and allow others to help us with them. The Spirit calls; the burdened need only heed the call.

There are three tenses of faith! When Lazarus died, Martha, his sister, said, "Lord, if You would have been here, my brother would not have died." This is historical faith. Its view is digressive. Then when Jesus said, "Lazarus will live again," his sister replied, "I know he will live in the resurrection." This is futuristic faith. It is progressive. Martha says, "But *even now* You have the power to raise him up again." (See John 11:21-27.) I feel 65 like Martha. Even now, after all you've been through, God has the power to raise you up again! This is the present tense of faith. Walk into your newness even now.

Chapter 6

ORIGINS OF FEMININITY

Nearly every home in America is wired for electricity. Walls are covered with receptacles which deliver the electric current. In order to take advantage of the power, something must be plugged into the receptacle. The receptacle is the female and the plug is the male.

Women were made like receptacles. They were made to be receivers. Men were made to be givers, physically, sexually and emotionally, and by providing for others. In every area, women were made to receive.

The woman was made, fashioned out of the man, to be a help meet. Through their union, they find wholeness in each other. She helps him meet and accomplish his task. In other words, if you have a power saw, it has great potential for cutting. However, it is ineffective until it is plugged in. The receptacle helps the power saw meet its purpose. Without that receptacle, the power saw, although mighty, remains limited.

However, there is a vulnerability about the receptacle. The vulnerability exists because they must be careful what kind of plug they are connected with. Receptacles are open. Women are open by nature and design. Men are closed. You must be careful what you allow to plug into you and draw strength from you. The wrong plugs may seek your help and drain your power.

God recognizes your vulnerability; therefore, He has designed that those who plug into a woman sexually will have a covenant with that woman. God never intended for humanity to have casual sex. His design always included the commitment of a covenant. He purposed that a man who has sexual relations with a woman would be committed to that same woman for life. Nothing short of this commitment meets His standard. God wants you covered like an outlet is covered, in order that no one tamper with your intended purpose. The married woman is covered by her husband. The single woman is covered by her chastity and morality. It is dangerous to be uncovered.

Originally, God created humanity perfect and good. "And God said, Let Us make man in Our image, after Our likeness: and let them have dominion over the fish of the sea, and over the fowl of the air, and over the cattle, and over all the earth, and over every creeping thing that creepeth upon the earth" (Gen. 1:26).

God placed Adam in the garden He had prepared for him. The only rule was man should not eat of the tree of the knowledge of good and evil. God wanted mankind to rely on Him for moral decisions. After the fall, history records the consequences of man trying to make moral decisions for himself.

Although God had made a wonderful place for Adam to live, the man remained less than complete. He needed a woman. Keep in mind, though, that she completed his purpose, not his person. If you're not complete as a person, marriage will not help you.

> And the Lord God caused a deep sleep to fall upon Adam, and he slept: and He took one of his ribs, and closed up the flesh instead thereof, and the rib, which the Lord God had taken from man, made He a woman, and brought her unto the man. Genesis 2:21-22

In Genesis chapter 3, we see that Eve allowed herself to be taken advantage of by satan, who plugged into her desire to see, taste and be wise. The enemy took advantage of her weakness. "And the man said, the woman whom Thou gavest to be with me, she gave me of the tree, and I did eat" (Gen. 3:12).

Eve had given her attention over to someone else. "And the Lord God said unto the woman, What is this that thou hast done? And the woman said, The serpent beguiled me, and I did eat" (Gen. 3:13). Adam's anger is shown by his statement, "You gave her to be with me." The woman answered, "Well, I couldn't help it. He plugged into me, or he beguiled me."

You've got to be careful who you let uncover you, because they can lead you to complete destruction. Notice what God did next:

And the Lord God said unto the serpent,
Because thou hast done this, thou art cursed
above all cattle, and above every beast of the
field; upon thy belly shalt thou go, and dust
shalt thou eat all the days of thy life: and I will
put enmity between thee and the woman, and
between thy seed and her seed; and it shall
bruise thy head, and thou shalt bruise his heel.
Genesis 3:14-15

There is a special enmity between femininity and the enemy. There is a special conflict between the woman and the enemy. That's why you must do spiritual warfare. You must do spiritual warfare against the enemy because you are vulnerable in certain areas and there is enmity between you and the enemy. You must be on your guard. Women tend to be more prayerful than men, once they are committed. If you are a woman living today, and you're not learning spiritual warfare, you're in trouble. The enemy may be taking advantage of you.

He is attracted to you because he knows that you were designed as a receptacle to help meet someone's vision. If he can get you to help meet his vision, you will have great problems. God said, "And I will put enmity between thee and the woman, and between thy seed and her seed" (Gen. 4:15a).

Now, God didn't say only "her seed and your seed." He said, "Between you and the woman." There is a fight between you and the devil. Who are the victims of the most rapes in this country? Who are the victims of the most child abuse? Who are the victims of much of the sexual discrimination in the job market? Who has the most trouble getting together, unifying with each other and collaborating? Over and over again, satan is attacking and assaulting your femininity.

Satan is continually attacking femininity. Mass populations of women have increased over the country. The Bible says that the time will come when there will be seven women to every one man (Is. 4:1) Statistics indicate that we are living in those times right now. Where you have more need than supply, there is growing enmity between the woman and the enemy.

If godly women do not learn how to start praying and doing effective spiritual warfare, they will not discern what is plugging into them. Perhaps you become completely vulnerable to moods and attitudes and dispositions. Perhaps you are doing things and you don't know why. Something's plugging into you. If you are tempted to rationalize, "I'm just in a bad mood. I don't know just what it is. I'm just evil. I'm tough," don't believe it. Something's plugging into you.

God wasn't finished with His pronouncements to the serpent after the fall. Next He addressed Eve directly.

Unto the woman He said, I will greatly multiply thy sorrow and thy conception; in sorrow thou shalt bring forth children; and thy desire shall be to thy husband, and he shall rule over thee. Genesis 3:16

God explained that birthing comes through sorrow. Everything you bring forth comes through pain. If it didn't come through pain, it probably wasn't worth much. If you're going to bring forth—and I'm not merely talking about babies, I'm talking about birthing vision and purpose—you will do so with sorrow and pain. If you're going to bring forth anything in your career, your marriage or your life, if you're going to develop anything in your character, if you're going to be a fruitful woman, it's going to come through sorrow. It will come through the things you suffer. You will enter into strength through sorrow.

Sorrow is not the object; it's simply the canal that the object comes through. Many of you are mistaking sorrow for the baby instead of the canal. In that case, all you have is pain. You ought to have a child for every sorrow. For every sorrow, for every intense groaning in your spirit, you ought to have something to show for it. Don't let the devil give you sorrow without seed. Any time you have sorrow, it is a sign that God is trying to get something through you and to you.

Be careful that you don't walk away with the pain and leave the baby in the store. You are the producers. You are the ones through whom life passes. Every child who enters into this world must come through you. Even Jesus Christ had to come through you to get legal entry into the world. He had to come through you. You are a channel and an expression of blessings. If there is to be any virtue, any praise, any victory, any deliverance, it's got to come through you.

Satan wants to use you as a legal entry into this world or into your family. That's how he destroyed the human race with the first family. He knows that you are the entrance of all things. You are the doors of life. Be careful what you let come through you. Close the doors to the planting of the enemy. Then know that when travail comes into your spirit, it's because you're going to give birth.

You will give birth! That's why you have suffered pain. Your spirit is signaling you that something is trying to get through. Don't become so preoccupied with the pain that you forget to push the baby. Sometimes you're pushing the pain and not the baby, and you're so engrossed with what's hurting you that you're not doing what it takes to produce fruit in your life.

When you see sorrow multiply, it is a sign that God is getting ready to send something to you. Don't settle for the pain and not get the benefit. Hold out. Disregard the pain and get the promise. Understand that God has promised some things to you that He wants you to have, and you've got to stay there on the table until you get to the place where you ought to be in the Lord. After all, the pain is forgotten when the baby is born.

What is the pain when compared with the baby? Some may have dropped the baby. That happens when you become so engrossed with the pain that you leave the reward behind you. Your attention gets focused on the wrong thing. You can be so preoccupied with how bad it hurts that you miss the joy of a vision giving birth.

Wouldn't it be a foolish thing for a woman to go into labor, go through all of the pain, stay on the delivery table, stay in labor for hours and hours, and simply get up and walk out of the hospital. It would be foolish for her to concentrate on the pain to the extent that she would leave the baby lying in the hospital. However, that is exactly what happens when you become preoccupied with how bad the past hurts you. Maybe you have walked away and left the baby lying on the floor.

For every struggle in your life, God accomplished something in your character and in your spirit. Why hold the pain and drop the baby when you could hold the baby and drop the pain? You are holding on to the wrong thing if all you do is concentrate on past pain. Release the pain. Pain doesn't fall off on its own. It's got to be released. Release the pain. Allow God to loose you from the pain, separate you from what has afflicted you and be left with the baby and not the problem.

He said, "In sorrow thou shalt bring forth children" (Gen. 3:16b). That includes every area of your life. That's in your character. That's true in your personality. It is true in your spirit as well as in your finances. Bring forth, ladies! If it comes into this world, it has to come through you. If you're in a financial rut, bring forth. If you're in need of healing for your body, bring forth. Understand that it must be brought forth. It doesn't just happen by accident.

The midwife tells a woman, "Push." The baby will not come forth if you don't push him. God will not allow you to become trapped in a situation without escape. But you've got to push while you are in pain if you intend to produce. I'm told that when the pain is at its height, that's when they instruct you to push—not when the pain recedes. When the pain is at its ultimate expression, that is the time you need to push.

As you begin to push in spite of the pain, the pain recedes into the background because you become pre-occupied with the change rather than the problem. Push! You don't have time to cry. Push! You don't have time to be suicidal. Push! This is not the time to give up. Push, because God is about to birth a promise through you. Cry if you must, and groan if you have to, but keep on pushing because God has promised that if it is to come into the world, it's got to pass through you.

There remains a conflict between past pain and future desire. Here is the conflict. He said, "...in sorrow thou shalt bring forth children; and thy *desire* shall be to thy husband, and he shall rule over thee" (Gen. 3:16). In other words, you have so much pain in producing the child that, if you don't have balance between past pain and future desire, you will quit producing. God says, "After the pain, your desire shall be to your husband." Pain is swallowed by desire.

Impregnated with destiny, women of promise must bear down in the spirit. The past hurts; the pain is genuine. However, you must learn to get in touch with something other than your pain. If you do not have desire, you

75

won't have the tenacity to resurrect. Desire will come back. After the pain is over, desire follows, because it takes desire to be productive again.

Chapter 7

A WOMB-MAN

I have been in the delivery room with my wife as she was giving birth. I witnessed the pain and suffering she endured. I believe that there were times of such intense pain that she would have shot me if she had had a chance. Her desire made her continue. She didn't simply give up. She endured the pain so new life could be born. Once the child was born, the pain was soon forgotten.

Until the desire to go forward becomes greater than the memories of past pain, you will never hold the power to create again. However, when the desire comes back into your spirit and begins to live in you again, it will release you from the pain.

God wants to give us the strength to overcome past pain and move forward into new life. Solomon wrote, "Where there is no vision, the people perish" (Prov. 29:18a). Vision is the desire to go ahead. Until you have a vision to go ahead, you will always live in yesterday's struggles. God is calling you to today. The devil wants you to live in yesterday. He's always telling you about what you cannot do. His method is to bring up your past. He wants to draw your attention backward.

God wants to put desire in the spirit of broken women. There wouldn't be any desire if there wasn't any relationship. You can't desire something that's not there. The very fact that you have a desire is in itself an indication that better days are coming. David said, "I had fainted, unless I had believed to see the goodness of the Lord in the land of the living" (Ps. 27:13). Expect something wonderful to happen.

When I was a boy, we had a dog named Pup. Don't let the name fool you, though. He was a mean and ferocious animal. He would eat anyone who came near him. We had him chained in the back of the house to a four-by-four post. The chain was huge. We never imagined that he could possibly tear himself loose from that post. He would chase something and the chain would snap him back. We often laughed at him, as we stood outside his reach.

One day Pup saw something that he really wanted. It was out of his reach. However, the motivation before him became more important than what was behind him. He pulled that chain to the limit. All at once, instead of drawing him back, the chain snapped, and Pup was loose to chase his prey.

That's what God will do for you. The thing that used to pull you back you will snap, and you will be liberated by a goal because God's put greatness before you. You can't receive what God wants for your life by looking back. He is mighty. He is powerful enough to destroy the yoke of the enemy in your life. He is strong enough to bring you out and loose you, deliver you, and set you free.

What we need is a seed in the womb that we believe is enough to produce an embryo. We must be willing to feed that embryo for it to grow and become visible. When it will not be hidden anymore, it will break forth in life as answered prayer. It will break forth. No matter how hard others try to hold it back, it will break forth.

Put the truth in your spirit and feed, nurture and allow it to grow. Quit telling yourself, "You're too fat, too old, too late, or too ignorant." Quit feeding yourself that garbage. That will not nourish the baby. Too often we starve the embryo of faith that is growing within us. It is unwise to speak against your own body. Women tend to speak against their bodies, opening the door for sickness and disease. Speak life to your own body. Celebrate who you are. You are the image of God.

Scriptures remind us of who we are. "I will praise Thee; for I am fearfully and wonderfully made: marvellous are Thy works; and that my soul knoweth right well" (Ps. 139:14). These are the words that will feed our souls. The truth will allow new life to swell up within us. Feed the embryo within with such words as these.

When I consider Thy heavens, the work of Thy
fingers, the moon and the stars, which Thou

hast ordained; what is man, that Thou art mindful of him? and the son of man, that Thou visitest him? Psalm 8:3-4

"And the Lord shall make thee the head, and not the tail; and thou shalt be above only, and thou shalt not be beneath" (Deut. 28:13a). "I can do all things through Christ which strengtheneth me" (Phil. 4:13). The Word of God will provide the nourishment that will feed the baby inside.

The Book of Hebrews provides us with a tremendous lesson on faith. When we believe God, we are counted as righteous. Righteousness cannot be earned or merited. It comes only through faith. We can have a good report simply on the basis of our faith. Faith becomes the tender, like money is the legal tender in this world that we use for exchange of goods and services. Faith becomes the tender, or the substance, of things hoped for, and the evidence of things not seen. By it the elders obtained a good report (Heb. 11:1-2).

"Through faith we understand that the worlds were framed by the word of God, so that things which are seen were not made of things which do appear" (Heb. 11:3). The invisible became visible and was manifested. God wants us to understand that just because we can't see it, doesn't mean that He won't do it. What God wants to do in us begins as a word that gets in the spirit. Everything that is tangible started as an intangible. It was a dream, a thought, a word of God. In the same way, what man has invented began as a concept in someone's mind. So just because we don't see it, doesn't mean we won't get it.

There is a progression in the characters mentioned in this chapter of Hebrews. Abel worshiped God by faith. Enoch walked with God by faith. You can't walk with God until you worship God. The first calling is to learn how to worship God. When you learn how to worship God, then you can develop a walk with God. Stop trying to get people to walk with God who won't worship. If you don't love Him enough to worship, you'll never be able to walk with Him. If you can worship like Abel, then you can walk like Enoch.

Enoch walked and by faith Noah worked with God. You can't work with God until you walk with God. You can't walk with God until you worship God. If you can worship like Abel, then you can walk like Enoch. And if you walk like Enoch, then you can work like Noah.

"But without faith it is impossible to please Him: for he that cometh to God must believe that He is, and that He is a rewarder of them that diligently seek Him" (Heb. 11:6). God will reward those who persevere in seeking Him. He may not come when you want Him to, but He will be right on time. If you will wait on the Lord, He will strengthen your heart. He will heal you and deliver you. He will lift you up and break those chains. God's power will loose the bands from around your neck. He will give you the garment of praise for the spirit of heaviness (Is. 61:3).

Abraham was a great man of faith. The writer of Hebrews mentions many areas of Abraham's faith. Abraham looked for a city whose builder and maker was God (11:10). However, he is not listed in the faith "hall of fame" as the one who produced Isaac. If Abraham was famous for anything, it should have been for producing Isaac. However, he is not applauded for that.

"Through faith also Sara herself received strength to conceive seed, and was delivered of a child when she was past age, because she judged Him faithful who had promised" (Heb. 11:11). When it comes to bringing forth the baby, the Scriptures do not refer to a man; they refer to a womb-man.

Sarah needed strength to conceive seed when she was past childbearing age. God met her need. She believed that He was capable of giving her a child regardless of what the circumstances looked like. From a natural perspective, it was impossible. The enemy certainly didn't want it to happen. God, however, performed His promise.

Why would you allow your vision to be incapacitated for the lack of a man? Many women have unbelieving husbands at home. Have faith for yourself. Be a womb-man. It doesn't matter whether someone else believes or not; you cling to the truth that He is doing a good work in you. Each of us needs our own walk with God. Stand back and thank God. Believe God and know that He is able to do it. Sarah didn't stand on her husband's faith; she stood on her own.

You are God's woman. You are not called to sit by the window waiting on God to send you a husband. You had better have some faith yourself and believe God down in your own spirit. If you would believe God, He would perform His Word in your life. No matter the desire or the blessing that you seek, God has promised to give you the desires of your heart. (Ps. 37:4)

Recognize that where life has seemed irrational and out of control, He will turn it around. When trouble was breaking loose in my life, and I thought I couldn't take it anymore, God intervened and broke every chain that held me back. He will do no less for you.

Abraham had many promises from God regarding his descendants. God told Abraham that his seed would be as the sands of the sea and the stars of Heaven (Gen. 22:17). There were two promises of seed given to Abraham. God said his seed would be as the sands of the earth. That promise represents the natural, physical nation of Israel. These were the people of the Old Covenant. However, God didn't stop there. He also promised that Abraham's seed would be as the stars of Heaven. These are the people of the New Covenant, the exalted people. That's the Church. We are exalted in Christ Jesus. We too are seed of Abraham. We are the stars of Heaven.

God had more plans for Abraham's descendants than to simply start a new nation on earth. He planned a new spiritual Kingdom that will last forever. The plan started as a seed, but it ended up as stars.

The only thing between the seed and the stars was the woman. Can you see why Sarah herself had to receive strength to conceive a seed when she was past childbearing age? Because the old man gave her a seed, she gave him the stars of Heaven. Whatever God gives you, He wants it to be multiplied in the womb of your spirit. When you bring it forth, it shall be greater than the former.

The enemy wants to multiply fear in your life. He wants you to become so afraid that you won't be able to figure out what you fear. You may be frightened to live in your own home. Some are afraid to correct their children. Some people fear standing up in front of others. Intimidated and afraid, many do not deliver a prophecy. God wants to set you free from fear as you are filled with faith.

In order to move forward, we must be willing to give up yesterday and go on toward tomorrow. We have to trust God enough to allow Him to come in and plow up our lives. Perhaps He needs to root out closet skeletons and replace them with new attitudes.

Sometimes women are so accustomed to being hurt that if anyone comes near them, they become defensive. Some may look tough and angry toward men, but God knows that behind that tough act, you are simply afraid. God deals directly with the issues of the heart and lets you know you do not have to be afraid. The plans of God are good. He is not like the people who have hurt and abused you. He wants only to help you be completely restored.

The enemy chains us to the circumstances of the past to keep us from reaching our potential. Satan has assigned fear to block up your womb. It blocks up your womb and causes you to be less productive than you like. He wants to destroy the spirit of creativity within you. God wants you to know that you have nothing to fear.

You can be creative. He will make you into the womb-man that He wants you to be.

Maybe you have been tormented and in pain. You have been upset. You have been frustrated. It is hindering your walk. God is releasing you from fear. "For God hath not given us the spirit of fear; but of power, and of love, and of a sound mind" (2 Tim. 1:7). You need to allow Him an opportunity in your life. Then you will start seeing beauty at all different stages of your life. Maybe you have been afraid of aging. God will give you the strength to thank Him for every year.

Although we must be careful not to become trapped by the past, we should look back and thank God for how He has kept us through the struggles. If you're like me, you will want to say, "I would never have made it if You had not brought me through." Celebrate who you have become through His assistance. In every circumstance, rejoice that He was with you in it.

I believe God is bringing health into dry bones, bones that were bowed over, bones that were bent out of shape, bones that made you upset with yourself. All are giving way to the life of the Spirit. Perhaps you responded to your history with low self-esteem. God will heal the inner wound and teach you how important you are to Him. You do make a difference. The world would be a different place if it were not for you. You are a part of His divine plan.

When the angel came to Mary and told her what God was going to do in her life, Mary questioned how it could be possible (Lk. 1:34). Perhaps God has been telling you things He wants to do in your life, but you have questioned Him. Perhaps your circumstance does not seem to allow you to accomplish much. Maybe you lack the strength to accomplish the task alone. Perhaps, like Mary, you are thinking only in the natural and that you must have a man to do God's will.

> *And the angel answered and said unto her, The*
> *Holy Ghost shall come upon thee, and the*
> *power of the Highest shall overshadow thee:*
> *therefore also that Holy Thing which shall be*
> *born of thee shall be called the Son of God.*
> Luke 1:35

If you have been wondering how God will make things come to pass in your life, remember that He will accomplish the task. No man will get the credit for your deliverance. He told Mary, "The Holy Ghost shall come upon thee." I believe the same is true of godly women today. The Holy Spirit will fill you. He will impregnate you. He will give life to your spirit. He will put purpose back into you. He will renew you. He will restore you.

God had a special plan for Mary. She brought forth Jesus. He has a special plan for us. We, however, aren't privileged to see the future. We don't know what kind of good things He has in store for us. But, He has a plan. God's women are to be womb-men. They are to be creative and bring forth new life. That is exactly what God wants to do with those who are broken and discouraged.

If great things came from those who never suffered, we might think that they accomplished those things of their own accord. When a broken person submits to God, God gets the glory for the wonderful things He accomplishes—no matter how far that person has fallen. The anointing of God will restore you and make you accomplish great and noble things. Believe it!

The hidden Christ that's been locked up behind your fears, your problems and your insecurity, will come forth in your life. You will see the power of the Lord Jesus do a mighty thing.

After the angel told Mary those words, do you know what she said? "And Mary said, Behold the handmaid of the Lord; be it unto me according to thy word. And the angel departed from her" (Lk. 1:38). "Be it unto me according to thy word." Not according to my marital status. Not according to my job. Not according to what I deserve. "Be it unto me according to thy word."

Mary knew enough to believe God and to submit to Him. She was taking an extreme risk. To be pregnant and unmarried brought dire consequences in those days. Yet she willingly gave herself over to the Lord.

Mary had a cousin named Elizabeth who was already expecting a child. The child in Elizabeth's womb was to be the forerunner of the Messiah. The two women came together to share their stories. When Elizabeth found a woman who would build her up, the Bible says that the baby leaped in her womb and she was filled with the Holy Ghost (Lk. 1:41).

The things you had stopped believing God for will start leaping in your spirit again. God will renew you. Often women have been working against each other, but God will bring you together. You will come together like Mary and Elizabeth. You will cause your babies to leap in your womb, and the power of the Lord Jesus will do a new thing in your life. The Holy Ghost will come upon you and restore you.

If you are a woman who has had a dream, and sensed a promise, reach out to Him. Every woman who knows that they have another woman inside them who hasn't come forth can reach their hearts toward God and He will meet those inner needs and cause them to live at their potential. He will restore what was stolen by your suffering and abuse. He will take back from the enemy what was swallowed up in your history.

He wants to bring you together, sisters. Every Mary needs an Elizabeth. He needs to bring you together. Stop your wars and fighting. Drop your guns. Throw down your swords. Put away your shields. God put something in your sister that you need. When you come together, powerful things will happen.

Satan attempts to keep us from our potential. He allows and causes horrible things to happen in lives so those lives will take on a different outlook. The fear of abuse can be removed only by the power of the Holy Spirit. There is great potential in women who believe. That potential may be locked up at times because of ruined histories. God will wipe the slate clean. He will likely use others to help in the process, but it is His anointing that will bring forth new life from deep within.

Chapter 8

Anoint Me...I'm Single!

Some of you do not understand the benefits of being single. In reality, while you're not married, you really ought to be involved with God. When you get married, you direct all of the training that you had while you were unmarried toward your spouse. The apostle Paul addressed this issue in his first letter to the church at Corinth.

> But I would have you without carefulness. He that is unmarried careth for the things that belong to the Lord, how he may please the Lord: but he that is married careth for the things that are of the world, how he may please his wife. There is difference also between a wife and a virgin. The unmarried woman careth for the things of the Lord, that she may be holy both in body and in spirit: but she that is married careth for the things of the

world, how she may please her husband. 1
Corinthians 7:32-34

Single women often forget some very important advantages they have. At five o'clock in the morning you can lie in bed and pray in the Spirit till seven-thirty, and not have to answer to anyone. You can worship the Lord whenever and however you please. You can lie prostrate on the floor in your house and worship and no one will become annoyed about it. "The unmarried woman careth for the things of the Lord."

Often those who minister in churches hear unmarried women complain about their need for a husband, but rarely does a single woman boast about the kind of relationship she is free to build with the Lord. Are you complaining about how you need someone? Take advantage of the time you don't have to worry about cooking meals and caring for a family. While a woman is single she needs to recognize that she has the unique opportunity to build herself up in the Lord without the drains that can occur later.

This time is in your life for you to charge up the battery cells. It's time to pamper; a time to take luxurious baths in milk and honey. You can lie there in the bath and worship the Lord. It's a ministry you have. Before you ask God for another man, take care of Him. If you are not ministering to His needs, and yet you are always before Him, asking Him to give you one of His princes to minister to, your prayers are not being heard because you are

not being faithful to Him. When you become faithful in

your singleness, then you will be better prepared to be faithful with a husband.

If you disregard the perfect husband, Jesus, you will certainly disregard the rest of us. If you ignore the one who provides oxygen, breath, bone tissue, strength, blood corpuscles, and life itself, you will certainly not be able to have regard for any earthly husband. The Lord wants to make sweet love to you. I'm not being carnal, I'm being real. He wants to hold you. He wants you to come in at the end of the day and say, "Oh, Lord, I could hardly make it today. Whew, I went through so much today. I'm so glad I have You in my life. They tried to devour me, but I thank You for this time we have together. I just couldn't wait to get alone and worship You and praise You and magnify You. You're the One who keeps me going. You're the lover of my soul, my mind, my emotions, my attitude and my disposition. Hold me. Touch me, strengthen me. Let me hold You. Let me bless You. I've set the night aside for us. Tonight is our night. I'm not so busy that I don't have time for You. For if I have no time for God, surely I have no time for a husband. My body is Yours. Nobody touches me but You. I am holy in body and in spirit. I am not committing adultery in our relationship. My body is Yours."

The Scripture calls unmarried women virgins because God is of the opinion that if you do not belong to a man, you belong strictly to Him. God thinks you are His. God's heart was broken with the ancient nation of Israel. It was broken because Israel came to Him and said, "Make us a king to judge us like all the nations" (1 Sam. 8:5). God had thought He was their King. When they preferred a man over Him, He gave them Saul, and Israel went to the dogs.

There is nothing wrong with wanting to be married. Simply take care of the Lord while you're waiting. Minister to Him. Let Him heal you and loose you, and worship Him. Single women ought to be the most consecrated women in the Church. Instead of singles being envious of married women, the married ought to be jealous of singles. You are the ones whose shadows ought to fall on people and they be healed. You are in a position and posture of prayer. The Lord has become your necessary food. While some married women are dependent on their husbands, single women learn to be dependent on the Lord. God has no limitations. A married woman may have a husband who can do some things, but God can do everything. What a privilege to be married to Him. He told Joel, "And upon the handmaids...will I pour out My spirit" (Joel 2:29). God has a special anointing for the woman who is free to seek Him. Her prayer life should explode in miracles!

That does not mean it is wrong for you to want physical companionship. God ordained that need. While you are waiting, though, understand that God thinks He's your husband. Be careful how you treat Him. He thinks He's your man. That's why He does those special favors for you. It is God who made you into a beautiful woman. He has been taking care of you, even when you didn't notice His provision. He is the source of every good thing. He keeps things running, and provides for your daily care. It is He who opened doors for you. He has been your edge, your friend and your companion.

Those who are married seek to please their spouse. Unmarried people seek to please the Lord. There is a special relationship of power between God and the single believer. Paul wrote, "Let every man abide in the same calling wherein he was called" (1 Cor. 7:20). In other words, the person who is single should be abiding, not wrestling, in singleness. Rather than spend all of our effort trying to change our position, we need to learn to develop the position where He has placed us. Isn't that what this means: "...I have learned, in whatsoever state I am, therewith to be content" (Phil. 4:11). I speak peace to you today.

Maybe you haven't been living like you really should. Maybe your house hasn't been the house of prayer that it really could have been. I want you to take this opportunity and begin to sanctify your house and body. Maybe your body has been mauled and pawed by all sorts of people. I want you to sanctify your body unto the Lord, and give your body as a living sacrifice to God (Rom. 12:1). If you can't keep your vow to God, you would never be able to keep your vow to a man. Give your body to God and sanctify yourself.

When God picks a wife for one of His royal sons, He will pick her from those who are faithful and holy unto Him. He may pass over those who didn't keep a vow to Him. If you will marry a king, he will have claimed you to be a queen. Begin to sanctify yourself. Bring your body before God. Bring your nature before God. Bring your passion to Him. Allow God to plug into your need.

Allow God to strengthen you until you can tell the devil, "My body belongs to God; my whole body belongs to God. I'm God's. And from the crown of my head to the soles of my feet, all that I am belongs to God. Early in the morning will I seek His face. I lie upon my bed at night and call on His name. I'll touch Him, embrace Him. He is the God of my salvation."

Marriage is ministry. If you are single, your ministry is directly unto the Lord. If you are married, your ministry is through your spouse. Then you learn how to be devoted to God through the relationship you have with your spouse.

Husbands, love your wives, even as Christ also loved the church, and gave Himself for it; that He might sanctify and cleanse it with the washing of the water by the word. Ephesians 5:25-26

Marriage is the place in human society where true love can be expressed in a great way. Marriage partners are to give self-sacrificially to one another. Jesus gave Himself for the Church. So also do husbands and wives give themselves to each other. Marriage is not a place where we seek self-gratification. It is the place where we seek to gratify another.

The sacredness of marriage is found in the relationship between Christ and the Church. Jesus continues to intercede on behalf of the Church, even after He gave His all for us. He is the greatest advocate of believers. He stands before God to defend and proclaim our value. Similarly, husbands and wives are to be bonded together to the extent that they become the greatest advocate of the other. Not demanding one's own way, but always seeking to please the other.

There can be no doubt that God has special plans for each one of us. The woman who is single needs to recognize her position and seek to please God in every way. "Single" means to be "whole." Enjoy being a whole person. The greatest visitation of the Holy Ghost in history happened to an unmarried woman named Mary. Before Joseph could, the Holy Ghost came upon her. That same life-giving anointing wants to come upon you. Stop murmuring and complaining. His presence is in the room! Worship Him! He is waiting on you.

Chapter 9

A Table for Two

So the Lord God caused the man to fall into a
deep sleep; and while he was sleeping, He took
one of the man's ribs and closed up the place
with flesh. Then the Lord God made a woman
from the rib he had taken out of the man, and
He brought her to the man.
Genesis 2:21-22 (NIV)

The first female mentioned in the Bible was created mature, without a childhood or an example to define her role and relationship to her husband. The first female was created a woman while Adam was asleep. That the Lord "brought her to the man" is the first hint of marriage. I believe it would be better if we still allowed God to bring to us what He has for us. The only biblical evolution I can find is the woman, who evolved out of man. She is God's gift to man. When God wanted to be praised, He created man in His own likeness and in His image. Likewise, God gave man someone like himself. Adam said that she is "bone of my bones, and flesh of my flesh" (Gen. 2:23). His attraction to her was her likeness to him. He called her "womb man" or woman. Like the Church of Christ, Eve was his body and his bride.

> *For no man ever yet hated his own flesh; but*
> *nourisheth and cherisheth it, even as the Lord*
> *the church: for we are members of His body, of*
> *His flesh, and of His bones. For this cause shall*
> *a man leave his father and mother, and shall be*
> *joined unto his wife, and they two shall be one*
> *flesh. This is a great mystery: but I speak con-*
> *cerning Christ and the church.*
> Ephesians 5:29-32

They were made of the same material. Adam says, "She is bone of my bone." He says nothing of her size, body build or hair color. These superficial components are like placing a product in an attractive container. The container may get the consumer to try it. But only the product will keep the consumer coming back. His attraction goes much deeper than externals. These outward attractions are certainly an advantage, but be assured that when it comes to marriage, no one ever stayed together simply because they were attractive. I don't know whether I agree with those who say there is only one person in the world for you. I would be afraid that, out of the billions of people on this planet, I wouldn't be able to find them. However, I do know that when you find a person with whom you are compatible, there is a bonding that consummates marriage and that has nothing to do with sex. I also understand how you could feel this person to be the only choice in the world. Let's face it, everyone you meet isn't bone of your bone! It is so important that you do not allow anyone to manipulate you into choosing someone with whom you have no bond. When Ezekiel speaks about the dry bones in the valley, he says, "The bones came together, bone to his bone" (Ezek. 37:7). Every person must pray and discern if the other is someone they could cleave to the rest of their life.

The term *cleave* is translated from the Hebrew word *debaq*. It means "to impinge, cling or adhere to; figuratively, to catch by pursuit or follow close after." There is a great need in most of our lives to cleave, to feel that this is where we belong. It is sad to realize our society has become so promiscuous that many have mistaken the thrill of a weekend fling for a knitting together of two thirsty hearts at the oasis of a loving commitment.

If you are reading this book and are not married, as you pray and seek God for companionship, consider these issues carefully. Find ten couples who have been married 12 years or more. Look at their wedding album. You will see that many of them have drastically changed. Realize that if those initial impressions were all that held a marriage together, these would already be over. Certainly, you owe it to your spouse and yourself to be all that you can. Still, there is much more involved in marriage than the superficial.

Marriage is so personal that no one will be able to stand outside your relationship and see why you bond with that person. If you are married, understand that your spouse isn't running for office. He shouldn't have to meet the approval of all your family and friends. Do not expect everyone to see what you see in each other; to cleave is to stick together. Have you made the commitment to stay together? The secret to cleaving is leaving. "For this cause shall a man *leave* his father and mother..." (Mk. 10:7). If you enter into marriage and still keep other options open, whether mental, emotional or physical, it will never work. When the tugging of adversity tries the bonds of your matrimony, you will fall apart. You must leave and cleave to your spouse. It is so unhealthy to cleave to someone other than your spouse for support. Now we all need wholesome friendships. However, none should have more influence over you than your spouse (after God). Some of you could save your marriages if you would leave some of these extra-marital ties and cleave to your companion!

It is not always a matter of feelings. We use this verse about other things, so why not about marriage? Romans 1:17 says, "For therein is the righteousness of God revealed from faith to faith: as it is written, The just shall live by faith." Believe God for your marriage! It will not be your feelings that heal your relationship; it will be your faith. Did you know that you cannot trust your own feelings? I counsel people all the time who sit with tears streaming down their weary faces and say, "I just can't trust him." I've got news for you. You can't trust yourself either! Your feelings will swing in and out. But your faith will not move. Cleaving implies that you don't want to get away. A marriage erodes like the banks of a river do—a little each day. There is a certain way a woman treats a man when she is fulfilled. It takes faith to treat a marriage that is frustrating with the same respect you would treat the prosperous relationship. I am simply saying many times you feel yourself holding back who you would like to be so you can maintain this strong exterior. Listen, do not allow another person to cause you to play a role that isn't really who you are. I realize that many of you may be in the middle of an awful relationship, but I can't counsel what I can't see. For specific needs, I recommend pastoral care and counseling. Nevertheless, I do want to warn you that suppressing the gentle side of you as a defense will not stop you from being hurt! If you suppress who you are, you will fall into depression! It is terrible to arrest who you are in an attempt to "fight fire with fire." The best way to fight fire is with water! The winning way of a woman is not in her words, it is in her character.

> *Wives, in the same way be submissive to your husbands so that, if any of them do not believe the word, they may be won over without words by the behavior of their wives, when they see the purity and reverence of your lives.* 1 Peter 3:1-2 (NIV)

> *For this is the way the holy women of the past who put their hope in God used to make themselves beautiful. They were submissive to their own husbands, like Sarah, who obeyed Abraham and called him her master. You are her daughters if you do what is right and do not give way to fear.* 1 Peter 3:5-6 (NIV)

Recently, while teaching a seminar, a lady raised her hand and said, "I am a widow. I lost my husband and he died unsaved." She was obviously wrestling with grief as she spoke. She continued, "I claimed First Peter 3:1 and at the end of his life he still was not saved." I responded, "That scripture doesn't mean that the responsibility of getting the husband saved rests on the wife. It just says that a submissive, quiet woman creates an atmosphere so he may be won." I rebuked the condemning spirit of guilt and she worshiped God under the anointing of the Holy Spirit. This passage of Peter's is not given to abuse women; it is given to instruct them about what works well in the home. Faith is not loud and fleshly; it is quiet and spiritual. Believe me when I say it is effective. No one can do anything to make another person be saved. You can't make them come home. You can't make someone love you. But you can create an atmosphere where your conduct is not undermining your prayers!

Women tend to be vocal while men tend to be physical. Women feel that everything needs to be discussed. Communication is crucial to a healthy relationship, it is just that men don't always talk with words. Men communicate through touch even in male to male relationships. A pat on the back, a two-handed handshake, means "I like you." Some think that men always communicate through sex. That isn't always the case. A coach playfully slaps a basketball player on the rump. He is not being sexual. He is saying, "Good job!" We must learn each other's method of communication. Instead of always feeling like you are neglected, ask your husband to share with you why he does what he does. Or better still, observe his method of communication and teach him yours. In all your getting, get understanding! It is terrible to be misunderstood! I am a giver. Whenever I feel affection, the first thing I want to do is buy a gift for my wife. I was shocked to find that although my wife will acknowledge the gifts, she will go into orbit over cards! To me this is insane! She keeps cards that are so old they've turned yellow. I read cards and enjoy them, but I seldom keep them. We spent the first few years of our marriage teaching each other our language.

Your spouse may really think he's telling you something that you keep complaining about not getting. He feels like "What more does she want? I told her that I married her. I did this and that and the other." You may be living in the Tower of Babel. That was the place where families divided because they could not understand each other's language. Sit down and learn each other's language before frustration turns your house into the Tower of Babel. At Babel all work ceased and arguing began. If you are arguing, it is because frustration exists between you. People who don't care don't argue. No one argues over what they would rather leave!

When you approach your husband, do not corner him. Catch him at a time when he won't feel interrogated. You would be surprised at how men tend to avoid open confrontation. I have seen big burly macho men intimidated about telling their 100-hundred pound wives they are going to do something they fear she will not like. Even men who are physically abusive still have moments when they feel anxiety about facing their wives. "It is better to dwell in the corner of the housetop, than with a brawling woman and in a wide house" (Prov. 25:24). Unless you are trying to drive him away, remember you could win the argument and still lose the man. Men's communication is different. I am not suggesting that men can't learn the communication method of their wives. I am merely saying that spouses must learn to appreciate each other's language. Remember, I briefly discussed faith for your marriage. Faith calls those things that are not as though they were (Rom. 4:17). Everything you were going to do for him when he changes, do it now and do it by faith. Then God will turn your Tower of Babel into a Pentecost! At Pentecost each person heard the message in their own language (Acts 2:6). I pray that God would interpret the language of your spouse and that your love be fruitful and productive.

> *And the Lord God called unto Adam, and said*
> *unto him, Where art thou? And he said, I heard*
> *Thy voice in the garden, and I was afraid,*
> *because I was naked; and I hid myself.*
> Genesis 3:9-10

Take it off—take it all off! No, not your clothes! It's the fig leaves that must go. Marriage is at its best when both parties can be naked and not be ashamed. It is important that your husband be able to take it off, to take it all off. There is no resting place for the man who hides in his own house. The Lord asked Adam, "Where art thou?" When men are restored to their rightful place in the home, the family will come out of chaos. Listen as Adam exposes the tendency of most men to avoid open confrontation. These are the four points of his confession: (a) I heard Thy voice. (b) I was afraid. (c) I was naked. (d) I hid myself. When you become confrontational, it's not that men don't hear you. But when men become afraid or exposed (naked), they have a tendency to hide. Marriage needs to be transparent. Fear will not heal, it will only hide. Both you and your spouse need to be able to expose your vulnerabilities without fear or condemnation. Woe to the man who has no place to lay his head.

> *And they were both naked, the man and his wife, and were not ashamed.* Genesis 2:25

I want to share something with you that may sound unorthodox. I pray it will bless someone. I want to stop by Delilah's house (Judg. 16:4-20). Most women would not want to stop at her house; most men would! Most men are not afraid of Delilah; most women do not like her. Her morals are inexcusable, but her methods are worth discussing. There are some things that every wife could learn, must learn, from Delilah. With all the colorful exegesis of our preachers who have described her as some voluptuous love goddess, they say she walked like a swinging pendulum, smelled like the richest incense and smiled like the glow of an exquisite candelabra. But, in actuality the Bible says nothing about her appearance. Her clothing, makeup or hairdo are not mentioned. What was it about this woman that was so powerful? What was it that attracted and captivated the attention of this mighty man, Samson? What was it about this woman that kept drawing him back to her arms? What was it about this woman that, when none of the warriors could get to Samson, the Philistine government put her on the payroll because of what she knew about men? What was it that made Samson keep going back to her bed even when he knew she was trying to kill him? He could not leave her alone—he desperately needed her. It is a "fatal attraction" in the Old Testament!

This discussion is for women married to men working in high-stress positions—men who are powerful and full of purpose; men who are the envy of everyone around them. Samson was that kind of man. Jesus described well the problem of highly motivated men. Jesus said, "Foxes have holes, and birds of the air have nests; but the Son of man hath not where to lay His head" (Lk. 9:58). Where can the mighty man lay his head? Where can he become vulnerable? Where can he take off his armor and rest for a few hours? He doesn't want to quit; he merely needs to rest. Is your home a restful place to be? Is it clean and neat? Is it warm and inviting? Delilah's place is ready. I am sure she has problems, but he doesn't have to solve them as soon as he comes home from fighting the enemy. She knows he is tired, so she says, "Come, lay your head in my lap."

I know we have pictured Delilah as being as lust-ridden as a porno star. But remember that the Bible doesn't even mention their sex life. I am sure that it was a factor. But Samson has had sex before. He had gotten up from the bed of the prostitute in Gaza and drove back the Philistines. He is not a high school boy whose mind is blown away by a new sexual idea. No, he is a mighty man. Wasn't it David who questioned at the demise of Saul, "How are the mighty fallen"? Well, tell David to ask Delilah, or if she is not at home, to ask Bathsheba! Delilah knew that all men are little boys somewhere deep inside. They are little boys who started their lives being touched by women. You sang their first song. You gave their first bath and when they were tired, they laid their weary heads against your warm breast and lapsed into sleep.

They listened at your silky voice calling them, "Momma's little man." You talked to them. You touched them and they felt safe in your arms—not criticized, not ostracized, just safe. Delilah stroked Samson. She talked to him. She gave him a place to lay his head. Even God inhabits the room of a praiser and allows the murmurer to wander. Men, created in the likeness of God, respond to praise. Praise will make a weary man perform. A woman who knows what to say to a man is difficult to withstand. For all men's tears and all their fears, they need your arms, your words, your song.

Marriage is a ministry. There is much more involved in it than selfish fulfillment. Love is centered around giving, not taking. When you marry someone, you marry everything he is and everything he has been. You inherit his strengths, fears and weaknesses. It is impossible to pick the parts you want and to leave the parts you don't. It is a package deal. God grants you the grace of ministering to your spouse, to the child in him. Don't be discouraged if you don't see immediate change. I want to remind you that it takes time even for a small cut to heal. Healing is a process and it takes time! God will give you the oil of compassion and the sweet wind of a sincere love to pour into the wounds of your husband.

But he that is married careth for the things that
are of the world, how he may please his wife.
There is difference also between a wife and a
virgin. The unmarried woman careth for the
things of the Lord, that she may be holy both
in body and in spirit: but she that is married

careth for the things of the world, how she may please her husband. 1 Corinthians 7:33-34

Marriage is so much a ministry that the apostle Paul teaches the married woman she cannot afford to become so spiritual that she is unavailable for the ministry of marriage. The Greek word used there for "careth" means to be anxious about or to have intense concern. God says, "I want the married woman to be concerned about pleasing her husband and vice versa." Many married women who spend a great deal of time fellowshiping with single women do not realize that their perspective and availability should be different. Your ministry, as a wife, begins not in the mall, not in the nursing home, but in your own home and to your own spouse. Now, I am certainly not implying that a woman should be locked in the kitchen and chained to the bed! I am sharing that priorities need to start in the home and then spread to careers, vocations and ministerial pursuits. For the woman who "careth for," God will anoint you to be successful in the ministry of marriage.

There will be no marriages in Heaven (Mt. 22:30). Marriage is for this world. Inasmuch as it is a worldly institution, married people cannot divorce themselves from the "things of the world." Notice this definition of the Greek word *kosmos* translated as "world" in our text:

Adorn, Adorning *kosmos* #2889 in *Strong's*, "a harmonious arrangement or order, then, adornment, decoration, hence came to denote the world, or the universe, as that which is Divinely arranged. The meaning 'adorning' is found in

1 Pet. 3:3. Elsewhere it signifies the world. Cp. *kosmios*, decent, modest, 1 Tim. 2:9; 3:2. See (World)" (*Vine's Expository Dictionary of Biblical Words*, Thomas Nelson Publishers, 1985).

It implies that there should be a concern for a harmonious order in the house. God gives the gift of marriage, but you must do your own decorating. Decorate your relationship or it will become bland for you and for your spouse. Decoration does not come where there is no concern. So God says, in effect, "I release the married woman from the level of consecration I expect from the single woman so she will be able to spend some time decorating her relationship." You have a ministry to your companion. I can hear someone saying, "That is good, but I need to spend time with the Lord." That is true. The Scripture didn't say married women were to be carnal. It just sets some priorities. Where there are no priorities, there is a sense of being overwhelmed by responsibility. You can still consecrate yourself as long as you understand you are called to be a companion to your spouse. God has ascribed honor to marriage. Your bed is undefiled. (See Hebrews 13:4.) However you choose to decorate your relationship is holy. Do not neglect each other in the name of being spiritual. God wants you to be together!

The husband should fulfill his marital duty to his wife, and likewise the wife to her husband. The wife's body does not belong to her alone but also to her husband. In the same way, the husband's body does not belong to him alone but also to his wife. Do not deprive each other

except by mutual consent and for a time, so
that you may devote yourselves to prayer.
Then come together again so that Satan will not
tempt you because of your lack of self-control.
1 Corinthians 7:3-5 (NIV)

If you are looking for someone to be your everything, don't look around, look up! God is the only One who can be everything. By expecting perfection from the flesh, you ask more out of someone else than what you can provide yourself. To be married is to have a partner: someone who is not always there or always on target or always anything! On the other hand, should you ever get in trouble and you don't know who to look to for help, you can count on your partner! It is to have someone to curl up against when the world seems cold and life uncertain. It is having someone who is as concerned as you are when your children are ill. It is having a hand that keeps checking your forehead when you aren't well. To be married is to have someone's shoulder to cry on as they lower your parent's body into the ground. It is wrapping wrinkled knees in warm blankets and giggling without teeth! To the person you marry you are saying, "When my time comes to leave this world and the chill of eternity blows away my birthdays and my future stands still in the night; it's your face I want to kiss good-bye. It is your hand I want to squeeze as I slip from time into eternity. As the curtain closes on all I have attempted to do and be; I want to look into your eyes and see that I mattered. Not what I looked like. Not what I did or how much money I made. Not even how talented I was. I want to look into the teary eyes of someone who loved me and see; I mattered!"

As I close this chapter, I hope you can relate to what a blessing it is to be alive, to be able to feel, to be able to taste life. Lift the glass to your mouth and drink deeply of life; it is a privilege to experience every drop of a human relationship. It is not perfect; like a suede jacket, the imperfection adds to its uniqueness. I am sure yours, like mine, is a mixing of good days, sad days and all the challenges of life. I hope you have learned that a truly good relationship is a spicy meal served on a shaky table, filled with dreams and pains and tender moments. Moments that, in those split-second flashbacks, make you smile secret smiles in the middle of the day. Moments so strong that they never die, but yet are so fragile they disappear like bubbles in a glass. It does not matter whether you have something to be envied or something to be developed; if you can look back and catch a few moments, or trace a smile back to a memory, you are blessed! You could have been anywhere doing anything but instead the maitre'd has seated you at a TABLE FOR TWO!

*C*hapter 10

DAUGHTER OF ABRAHAM

I believe it is important that women get healed and released in their spirits. I'm excited about what God is doing. I believe that God will move freshly in the lives of women in an even greater way.

God knows how to take a mess and turn it into a miracle. If you're in a mess, don't be too upset about it because God specializes in fixing messes. God is saying some definite things about women being set free and delivered to fulfill their purpose in the Kingdom.

Let's look once again at the infirm woman of the Gospel of Luke, chapter 13:

> *And He was teaching in one of the synagogues*
> *on the sabbath. And, behold, there was a*
> *woman which had a spirit of infirmity eighteen*
> *years, and was bowed together, and could in*
> *no wise lift up herself. And when Jesus saw*

*her, He called her to Him, and said unto her,
Woman, thou art loosed from thine infirmity.
And He laid His hands on her: and immediately she was made straight, and glorified God.
And the ruler of the synagogue answered with
indignation, because that Jesus had healed on
the sabbath day, and said unto the people,
There are six days in which men ought to
work: in them therefore come and be healed,
and not on the sabbath day. The Lord then
answered him, and said, Thou hypocrite, doth
not each one of you on the sabbath loose his ox
or his ass from the stall, and lead him away to
watering? And ought not this woman, being a
daughter of Abraham, whom satan hath
bound, lo, these eighteen years, be loosed from
this bond on the sabbath day? And when He
had said these things, all His adversaries were
ashamed: and all the people rejoiced for all the
glorious things that were done by Him.*
Luke 13:10-17

When the Lord gets through working on you, all
your adversaries will be ashamed. All your accusers will
be ashamed of themselves. All the people who contrib-
uted to your sense of low self-esteem will be ashamed
when God gets through unleashing you. You won't have
to prove anything. God will prove it. He will do it in your
life. When He gets through showing that you've done the
right thing and come to the right place, they will drop
their heads and be ashamed.

We have already shown how this woman was so bound by satan for 18 years that she could not even straighten herself up. She had a past that tormented her, but Jesus set her free. He unleashed her potential that satan had bound up.

Many women in the Church have not really seen Christ as the answer to their dilemma. They go to church, they love the Lord, they want to go to Heaven when they die, but they still do not see Christ as the solution to their problem. Often we try to separate our personal life from our spiritual life. Many see Jesus as a way to Heaven and the solution to spiritual problems, but they fail to see that He is the solution to all of life's problems.

Can you imagine how hard life was for that woman who was bowed over? She had to struggle, because of her problem, to come to Jesus. Few of us are crippled in the same way. However, we all face crippling limitations. We can be bowed over financially. We can be bowed over emotionally. We can be bowed over where we have no self-esteem. He wants to see us struggling toward Him. Jesus could have walked to this woman, but He chose not to. He wants to see us struggle toward Him.

He wants you to want Him enough to overcome obstacles and to push in His direction. He doesn't want to just throw things at you that you don't have a real conviction to receive. When you see a humped-over person crawling through the crowd, know that that person really wants help. That kind of desire is what it takes to change your life. Jesus is the answer.

I may seek help by going from one person to another, but only He is the answer. I may be sick in my body, but He is the answer. If my son is dead, or insane on drugs, and I need Him to resurrect my child, He is the answer. If I am having family problems with my brother who is in trouble, He's the answer. It doesn't matter what the problem is, He is the answer.

Jesus touched this woman. There's a place in God where the Lord will touch you and provide intimacy in your life when you're not getting it from other places. You must be open to His touch. If you can't receive from Him, you may find yourself like the woman at the well, who sought physical gratification (John 4:18). If you seek only the physical when you really need intimacy, what you end up getting is simply sex. Sex is a poor substitute for intimacy. It's nice with intimacy, but when it is substituted for intimacy, it's frustrating.

Jesus knew this woman. He was the only one who truly knew her. He touched her and healed her. He unleashed her potential that had been bound for 18 years. You can accomplish everything once you have been called to Jesus. From that moment on you become invincible.

However, most likely your words have hindered you. Often we are snared by the words in our own mouth. The enemy would love to destroy you with your own words. Satan has turned your back against you. He will use your strength against you. Many of you have beat yourself down with the power of your own words. You have twisted your own back. The enemy worked you against yourself until you saw yourself as crippled.

118

Reverse his plan. If you had enough force to bend your-self, you've got enough force to straighten yourself back up again.

The Lord told this woman the truth about herself. He told her that she was loosed and set free. He saw the truth despite what everyone else saw. She was important.

The religious critics didn't like what Jesus had done. His power showed how powerless their religion was. They accused Him of breaking the law by performing a miracle on the Sabbath day. Christ acknowledged their hypocrisy by addressing a common occurrence in the area. They all valued their livestock, He said. Then He reminded them that they would loose their ass on the Sab-bath so that it could get a drink. Surely this woman was more valuable than any animal. She could be loosed from her pain and sickness regardless of the day.

Sometimes pain can become too familiar. Ungodly relationships often become familiar. Change doesn't come easily. Habits and patterns are hard to break. Sometimes we maintain these relationships because we fear change. However, when we see our value the way Jesus sees us, we muster the courage to break away.

He is your defense. He will defend you before your critics. Now is the time for you to focus on receiving the miraculous and getting the water that you could not get before. He is loosing you to water. You haven't been drinking for 18 years, but now you can get a drink. With Jesus, you can do it.

Have you been a beast of burden? Some of you have been a pack horse for many years. People have dumped on you. You've had to grit your teeth. You've never been allowed to develop without stress and weights, not just because of the circumstances, but because of how deeply things effect you. Our God, however, is a liberator.

The Lord is my light and my salvation; whom shall I fear? the Lord is the strength of my life; of whom shall I be afraid? When the wicked, even mine enemies and my foes, came upon me to eat up my flesh, they stumbled and fell. Though an host should encamp against me, my heart shall not fear: though war should rise against me, in this will I be confident. One thing have I desired of the Lord, that will I seek after; that I may dwell in the house of the Lord all the days of my life, to behold the beauty of the Lord, and to inquire in His temple. Psalm 27:1-4

You must reach the point where it is the Lord whom you desire. Singleness of heart will bring about deliverance. Perhaps you have spent all your time and effort trying to prove yourself to someone who is gone. Maybe an old lover left you with scars. The person may be dead and buried, but you are still trying to win his approval.

In this case, you are dedicated to worthless tasks. You are committed to things, unattainable goals, that will not satisfy. Christ must be your ambition.

Luke 13:13b reads, "And immediately she was made straight, and glorified God." Christ dealt with 18 years of torment in an instant. One moment with Jesus, and immediately she was well. For some things you don't have time to recover gradually. The moment you get the truth, you are loosed. Immediately she recovered.

Once you realize that you have been unleashed, you will feel a sudden change. When you come to Jesus, He will motivate you. You will see that other woman in you. You need to blossom and bring her forth.

Notice the sixteenth verse of Luke 13. "And ought not this woman, being a daughter of Abraham, whom satan hath bound, lo, these eighteen years, be loosed from this bond on the sabbath day?" He called her, "a daughter of Abraham." She may have been bent over, but she was still Abraham's daughter. Don't let your condition negate your position.

She was unleashed because of who her father was. It had little to do with who she was. The Bible doesn't even mention her name. We will never know who she was until we reach Heaven. Although we don't know who she was, we know whose she was. She was a daughter of Abraham.

Faith is an equal opportunity business. There is no discrimination in it. Faith will work for you. When you approach God, don't worry about the fact that you are a woman. Never become discouraged on that basis when it comes to seeking Him. You will only get as much from God as you can believe Him for.

You won't be able to convince Him, seduce Him, break Him down, or trick Him. God will not move because you cry and act melancholy. Now, you may move me like that. Certainly that works with men, but not with God. God only accepts faith, not just feminine rhetoric, not hysteria—just plain old faith in God.

He wants you to believe Him. He wants you to personalize the truth that you can do all things through Him (Phil. 4:13). He is trying to teach you so when the time for a real miracle does come, you'll have some faith to draw from. God wants you to understand that if you can believe Him, you can go from defeat to victory and from poverty to prosperity!

Faith is more than a fact—faith is an action. Don't tell me you believe when your actions do not correspond with your conviction. If your actions don't change, you might still think you are tied. When you finally understand that you are loose, you will start behaving as if you were set free.

When you are loose, you can go anywhere. If I had one end of a rope around my neck, I would only be able to walk the length of the rope. Once I am unleashed from that rope, I can walk as far as I want. You are whole; you are loose. You can go anywhere.

Hebrews chapter 11 is a faith "hall of fame." It lists great people of God who believed Him and accomplished great exploits. Abraham is given tremendous attention in this chapter. He is revered by millions as the father of faith. He is the first man in history to believe God to the point where it was counted as righteousness. He was saved by faith. Jesus said that the infirm woman was a daughter of Abraham. She was worthy. She had merit because she was Abraham's descendant and had faith.

There are two contrasting women mentioned in the faith "hall of fame." Sarah, Abraham's wife, is listed. Rahab, the Jericho prostitute, is listed as well. A married woman and a whore made it to the hall of fame. A good clean godly woman and a whore made it into the book. I understand how Sarah was included, but how in the world did this prostitute get to be honored? She was listed because God does not honor morality. He honors faith. That was the one thing they had in common; nothing else.

The Bible doesn't talk about Rahab having a husband. She had the whole city. Sarah stayed in the tent and knit socks. She moved wherever her husband went and took care of him. There was no similarity in their life styles, just in their faith. God saw something in Sarah that He also saw in Rahab. Do not accept the excuse that because you have lived like a Rahab you can't have the faith experience.

God wants you to believe Him. Make a decision and stand on it. Rahab decided to take a stand on the side of God's people. She hid the spies. She made the decision based on her faith. She took action. Faith is a fact and faith is an action. She took action because she believed God would deliver her when Jericho fell to the Israelites.

Sarah received strength to carry and deliver a child when she was well past childbearing age. She took action because she judged Him faithful who had promised (Heb. 11:11). She went through the birth process and delivered a child not because of her circumstance, but because of her faith. She believed God.

God wants your faith to be developed. Regardless of your position and your past, God raises people up equally. Faith is an equal opportunity business. No matter how many mistakes you have made, it is still faith that God honors. You see, you may have blown it, but God is in the business of restoring broken lives. You may have been like Rahab, but if you can believe God, He will save your house. You know, He didn't save only her. He saved her entire household. All the other homes in Jericho were destroyed. The only house God saved in the city was the house where the prostitute lived.

You would have thought He would have saved some nice little lady's house. Perhaps He would have saved some cottage housing an old woman, or a little widow's house, with petunias growing on the sidewalk. No, God saved the whore's house. Was it because He wanted it? No, He wanted the faith. That is what moves God.

If you believe that your background will keep you from moving forward with God, then you don't understand the value of faith. The thing God is asking from you is faith. Some may live good, clean, separated lives; maybe you are proud of how holy you are. He still honors only faith.

If you want to grasp the things of God, you will not be able to purely because of your life style, but because of your conviction. God gave healing to some folks who weren't even saved. They were sinners. Perhaps some of them never did get saved, but they got healed because they believed Him. The thing that moves God is faith. If you believe Him, He will move in your life according to your faith and not to your experience. There was something in Rahab's house that God called valuable. Faith was there. God protected her from the fire.

He also saved her things. When the fire was over, Rahab was the richest woman in the city. She was the only woman left in town that owned property. So He will save your finances. You must simply believe Him.

There were a group of sisters in the Old Testament who proved that God was interested in what happens to women.

> Then came the daughters of Zelophehad, the son of Hepher, the son of Gilead, the son of Machir, the son of Manasseh, of the families of Manasseh, the son of Joseph: and these are the names of his daughters; Mahlah, Noah, and Hoglah, and Milcah, and Tirzah. And they stood before Moses, and before Eleazar the priest, and before the princes and all the congregation, by the door of the tabernacle of the congregation, saying, Our father died in the wilderness, and he was not in the company of them that gathered themselves together against the Lord in the company of Korah; but died in his own sin, and had no sons. Numbers 27:1-3

There were a group of women who were left alone. There were no men left in the family. Their father had wealth, but he had no sons. Prior to this time, women were not allowed to own property or to have an inheritance except through their husbands. Only men could own property.

They continued with their appeal. "Why should the name of our father be done away from among his family, because he hath no son? Give unto us therefore a possession among the brethren of our father" (Num. 27:4).

They appealed to Moses for help on the basis of who their father was. They stated their case and looked to him as God's authority. They couldn't understand why they should not have some of their father's wealth simply because they were born female. Their uncles would have received all their father's wealth. They would have been poor and homeless, receiving only leftovers from others. However, these women were daughters of Abraham. If you want the enemy to release you, remind him whose daughter you are.

No one would have listened to them if they had not initiated a meeting to plead their case. Perhaps you who have struggled need to call a meeting. Get in touch with people in power and demand what you want, or you will not get it. Speak for yourself. They could not understand why they were being discriminated against because of their gender.

One of the reasons Zelophehad's daughters could make a proper case for themselves was they were right. It was time to teach God's people that women have value. Abraham's daughters have worth. They didn't wait for a man to defend them; they took action in faith. God saw faith in those women.

> *And Moses brought their cause before the*
> *Lord. And the Lord spake unto Moses, saying,*
> *The daughters of Zelophehad speak right: thou*
> *shalt surely give them a possession of an inher-*
> *itance among their father's brethren; and thou*
> *shalt cause the inheritance of their father to*
> *pass unto them.* Numbers 27:5-7

Moses didn't know what to do, so he asked God. The women were vindicated. If they had failed, surely they would have been scorned by all the good people of Israel who would have never challenged Moses in such a way. Instead they received the wealth of their father. God is no respecter of persons. Faith is based on equal opportunity.

Like the infirm woman, you are a daughter of Abraham if you have faith. You want the inheritance of your father to pass on to you. Why should you sit there and be in need when your Father has left you everything? Your Father is rich, and He left everything to you. However, you will not get your inheritance until you ask for it. Demand what you father left you. That degree has your name on it. That promotion has your name on it. That financial breakthrough has your name on it.

There is no need to sit around waiting on someone else to get you what is yours. Nobody else is coming. The One who needed to come has already come. Jesus said, "I am come that they might have life, and that they might have it more abundantly" (Jn. 10:10b). That is all you need.

The power to get wealth is in your tongue. You shall have whatever you say. If you keep sitting around murmuring, groaning and complaining, you use your tongue against yourself. Your speech has got you bent over and crippled. You may be destroying yourself with your words.

Open your mouth and speak something good about yourself so you can stand up on your feet. You used your mouth against yourself. Then you spoke against all the other women around you because you treated them like you treated yourself. Open your mouth now and begin to speak deliverance and power. You are not defeated. You are Abraham's daughter.

When you start speaking correctly, God will give you what you say. You say you want it. Jesus said, "And all things, whatsoever ye shall ask in prayer, believing, ye shall receive" (Mt. 21:22). God willed you something. Your Father left you an inheritance. If God would bless the sons of Abraham, surely He would bless the daughters of Abraham.

God will give you whatever you ask for (Jn. 14:13). God will give you a business. God will give you a dream. He will make you the head and not the tail (Deut. 28:13). God's power brings all things up under your feet. Believe him for your household. God will deliver. You don't need a sugar daddy. You have the Jehovah-jireh, the best provider this world has ever known.

"For ye are all the children of God by faith in Christ Jesus" (Gal. 3:26). Women are just as much children of God as men are. Everything that God will do for a man, He will do for a woman. You are not disadvantaged. You can get an inheritance like any man. Generally men don't cry about being single—they simply get on with life and stay busy. There is no reason a woman can't be complete in God without a husband.

If you choose to get married, you should get married for the right reasons. Don't give in to a desperate spirit that forces you to put up with someone less than what you would want. You could become stuck with someone immature and bear three little boys. Then you would have four little boys. That is no way to live. You need someone who has some shoulders and backbone.

You need to marry someone who will hold you, help you, strengthen you, build you up, and be with you when the storms of life are raging. If you want a cute man, buy a photograph. If you want some help, marry a godly man.

For as many of you as have been baptized into Christ have put on Christ. There is neither Jew nor Greek, there is neither bond nor free, there is neither male nor female: for ye are all one in Christ Jesus. Galatians 3:27-28

Those ancient Israelite women, the daughters of Zelophehad, thought it was a disgrace for them to be starving when they considered who their father was. Rahab was a harlot until she found faith. Once she had faith, she no longer turned to her old profession. The infirmed woman was bowed over until Jesus touched her. Once He touched her, she stood up. You have put on Christ. There is no reason to be bent over after His touch. You can walk with respect even when you have past failures. It's not what people say about you that makes you different. It is what you say about yourself, and what your God has said about you, that really matters.

Just because someone calls you a tramp doesn't mean you have to act like one. Rahab walked with respect. You will find her name mentioned in the lineage of Jesus Christ. She went from being a prostitute to being one of the great-grandmothers of our Lord and Savior Jesus Christ. You can't help where you've been, but you can help where you're going.

God is not concerned about race. He is not concerned about your being Black. You may think, " My people came over on a boat and picked cotton on a plantation." It doesn't make any difference. The answer isn't to be White. Real spiritual advantage does not come from the color of your skin. It's not the color of your skin that will bring deliverance and help from God; it's the contents of your heart.

Some of us have particular problems based on where we came from. We've got to deal with it. God says there is neither Greek nor Jew. There is no such thing as a Black church. There is no such thing as a White church. It's only one Church, purchased by the blood of the Lamb. We are all one in Christ Jesus.

You may have been born with a silver spoon in your mouth too, but it doesn't make any difference. In the Kingdom of God, social status doesn't mean anything. Rahab can be mentioned right next to Sarah because if you believe, God will bless. Faith is the only thing in this world where there is true equal opportunity. Everyone can come to Jesus.

"There is neither male nor female" (Gal. 3:28). God doesn't look at your gender. He looks at your heart. He doesn't look at morality and good works. He looks at the faith that lives within. God is looking in your heart. You are spirit, and spirits are sexless. That's why angels don't have sexes; they simply are ministering spirits. Don't think of angels in terms of gender. They can manifest themselves as men, but angels are really ministering spirits. All people are one in Christ Jesus.

Christ saw the worth of the infirm woman because she was a daughter of Abraham. She had faith. He will unleash you also from the pain you have struggled with and the frustrations that have plagued you. Faith is truly equal opportunity. If you will but dare to believe that you are a daughter of Abraham, you will find the power to stand up straight and be unleashed. The potential that has been bound will then truly be set free.

Chapter 11

A WOMAN WITHOUT EXCUSE

Attitudes affect the way we live our lives. A good attitude can bring success. A poor attitude can bring destruction. An attitude results from perspective. I'm sure you understand what perspective is. Everyone seems to have a different perspective. It comes from the way we look at life, and the way we look at life is often determined by our history.

The events of the past can cause us to have an outlook or perspective on life that is less than God's perspective. The little girl who was abused learns to defend herself by not trusting men. This attitude of defensiveness often stretches into adulthood. If we have protected ourselves a certain way in the past with some measure of success, then it is natural to continue that pattern throughout life. Unfortunately, we often need to learn how to look past our perspective and change our attitudes.

The infirm woman whom Jesus healed was made completely well by His touch. She couldn't help herself no matter how hard she tried, but Jesus unleashed her. He lifted a heavy burden from her shoulders and set her free.

Today, many of us have things we need to be separated from or burdens we need lifted. We will not function effectively until those things are lifted off of us. We can function to a certain point under a load, but we can't function as effectively as we would if the thing was lifted off of us. Perhaps some of you right now have things that are burdening you down.

You need to commend yourselves for having the strength to function under pressure. Unfortunately, we often bear the weight of it alone, since we don't feel free to tell anyone about our struggles. So whatever strides you have made, be they large or small, you have made them against the current.

It is God's intention that we be set free from the loads we carry. Many people live in co-dependent relationships. Others are anesthetized to their problems because they have had them so long. Perhaps you have become so accustomed to having a problem that even when you get a chance to be delivered, you find it hard to let it go. Problems can become like a security blanket.

Jesus took away this woman's excuse. He said, "Woman, thou art loosed from thine infirmity." The moment He said that, it required something of her that she hadn't had to deal with before. For 18 years she could excuse herself because she was handicapped.

The moment He told her the problem was gone, she had no excuse.

Before you get out of trouble, you need to straighten out your attitude. Until your attitude is corrected, you can't be corrected.

Why should we put up all the ramps and rails for the handicapped if we can heal them? You want everyone to make an allowance for your problem, but your problem needs to make an allowance for God and to humble itself to the point where you don't need special help. I'm not referring to physical handicaps; I'm addressing the emotional baggage that keeps us from total health. You cannot expect the whole human race to move over because you had a bad childhood. They will not do it. So you will end up in depression and frustration, and even confusion. You may have trouble with relationships because people don't accommodate your hang-up.

One woman I pastored was extremely obnoxious. It troubled me deeply, so I took the matter to God in prayer. The Lord allowed me to meet her husband. When I saw how nasty he talked to her, I understood why, when she reached down into her reservoir, all she had was hostility. That's all she had taken in. You cannot give out something that you haven't taken in.

Christ wants to separate you from the source of your bitterness until it no longer gives you the kind of attitude that makes you a carrier of pain. Your attitude affects your situation—your attitude, not other people's attitude about you. Your attitude will give you life or death.

One of the greatest deliverances people can ever experience in life is to have their attitude delivered. It doesn't do you any good to be delivered financially if your attitude doesn't change. I can give you five thousand dollars, but if your attitude, your mental perspective, doesn't change, you will be broke in a week because you'll lose it again. The problem is not how much you have, it's what you do with what you have. If you can change your attitude, you might have only 50 dollars, but you'll take that 50 and learn how to get 5 million.

When God comes to heal, He wants to heal your emotions also. Sometimes all we pray about is our situation. We bring God our shopping list of desires. Fixing circumstances is like applying a band-aid, though. Healing attitudes set people free to receive wholeness.

The woman who was crippled for 18 years was delivered from her infirmity. The Bible says she was made straight and glorified God. She got a new attitude. However, the enemy still tried to defeat her by using the people around her. He does not want to let you find health and strength. He may send another circumstance that will pull you down in the same way if you don't change your attitude.

When you first read about this woman, you might have thought that the greatest deliverance was her physical deliverance. I want to point out another deliverance that was even greater. The Bible said that when the Lord laid His hand on her, she was made straight. That's physical deliverance. Then her attitude changed. She entered into praise and thanksgiving and worshiped the Lord.

This woman began to leap and rejoice and magnify God and shout the victory like anybody who has been delivered from an 18-year infirmity should. While she was glorifying God over here, the enemy was stirring up strife over there. She just kept on glorifying God. She didn't stop praising God to answer the accusers.

The Lord is your defense. You do not have to defend yourself. When God has delivered you, do not stop what you're doing to answer your accusers. Continue to bless His name, because you do not want your attitude to become defensive. When you have been through difficult times, you cannot afford to play around with moods and attitudes. Depression and defensiveness may make you vulnerable to the devil.

This woman had to protect herself by entering into defensive praise. This was not just praise of thanksgiving, but defensive praise. Defensive praise is a strategy and a posture of war that says, "We will not allow our attitude to crumble and fall."

When you get to the point that you quit defending yourself or attacking others, you open up a door for the Lord to fight for you.

When this woman began to bless God, she built walls around her own deliverance. She decided to keep the kind of attitude that enabled the deliverance of God to be maintained in her life. When you have been through surgery, you cannot afford to fool around with band-aids.

When you're in trouble, God will reach into the mess and pull you out. However, you must be strong enough not to let people drag you back into it. Once God unleashes you, don't let anyone trap you into some religious fight. Keep praising Him. For this woman, the more they criticized her, the more she was justified because she just stood there and kept believing God. God is trying to get you to a place of faith. He is trying to deliver you from an attitude of negatives.

When you have had problems for many years, you tend to expect problems. God must have healed this woman's emotions also because she kept praising Him instead of paying attention to the quarrel of the religious folks around her. She could have easily fallen into negative thinking. Instead, she praised God.

Can you imagine what would have happened if she had stopped glorifying God and started arguing? If an argument could have gotten through her doors, this whole scene would have ended in a fight. But she was thankful and determined to express her gratitude.

The Lord wants to speak a word of faith to you. He wants to set you free from every power that has kept you in bondage. In order for that to be received in your spirit, you must allow Him to come in and instill faith. The emotional walls that surround us have to come down.

Love is eternal. It is not limited by time. When you commit yourself to loving someone, you make that commitment to all the person is. You are who you are because of your history. For me, that means I love my wife and who she has become. But in order for me to love her effectively, she must allow me into her history.

Many couples in a relationship argue over relatively insignificant things. Often the reason these things are important is one or the other is reminded of a past event. How can one person love another if he or she doesn't know the other person's history?

The Church has become too narrow in its approach to attitude. We want to keep our attitudes to ourselves and simply take them to God. Although we certainly should take them to Him, we also need to learn to "bear ye one another's burdens" (Gal. 6:2a).

Thousands walk in fear. The Church can give strength to counter that fear. Thousands have built a wall around them because they do not trust anyone else. The Church can help its members learn to trust one another. Thousands are co-dependent and get their value from a relationship with another person. The Church can point to God's love as the source for self-worth. We are not valuable because we love God; we are valuable because He loves us.

Jesus took away the ability of the infirm woman to make excuses for herself and gave her the strength to maintain an attitude of gratitude and praise. The Church today is to be the kind of safe haven that does the same thing. Those who are wounded should be able to come and find strength in our praise.

139

Gratitude and defensive praise is contagious. Although the Bible doesn't specifically say so, I imagine that those who saw what was going on the day Jesus healed the infirm woman were caught up in praise as well. The Church also must find room to join in praise when the broken are healed. Those who missed the great blessing that day were those who decided to argue about religion.

The Bible describes Heaven as a place where the angels rejoice over one sinner who comes into the faith (Lk. 15:10). They rejoice because Jesus heals those who are broken. Likewise God's people are to rejoice because the brokenhearted and emotionally wounded come to Him.

Christ unleashed power in the infirm woman that day. He healed her body and gave her the strength of character to keep a proper attitude. The woman who is broken and wounded today will find power unleashed within her too when she responds to the call and brings her wounds to the Great Physician.

Chapter 12

THE TRUE BEAUTY OF A WOMAN

We are fascinated with beauty. There are contests of all kinds to determine who is the most beautiful of all. Advertisers spend millions of dollars to promote beauty pageants. The beauty industry is one of the largest in America. Women spend huge amounts of money on makeup, fashionable clothing, and jewelry. Plastic surgeons are kept busy cutting and tucking extra flesh and reshaping features to make people more attractive.

In spite of all this attention, what is the true beauty of a woman? What is it that makes her genuinely attractive? Many feel unattractive because they don't meet a certain image to which they have aspired. Others are constantly frustrated in trying to get someone to notice their attractiveness.

No scientist has ever been able to make a woman. No doctor has been able to create a woman. No engineer has been able to build a woman. However, God has made fine women. You don't have to look like a TV commercial to be beautiful. No one stays 21 forever.

We must learn to thank God for who we are. Don't be a silly woman watching television and crying because she doesn't look like the girl who opened up the window in the game show. You are not supposed to look like that. If God had wanted you to look like that, He would have made you like that. God will send somebody along who will appreciate you the way you are.

While waiting on that person, start appreciating yourself. Remind yourself, "I am valuable to God. I am somebody. And I won't let another use me and abuse me and treat me like I'm nothing. Yes, I've been through some bad times. I've been hurt and I've been bent out of shape, but the Lord touched me and loosed me and now I am glorifying God and I'm not going back to where I came from."

As I mentioned earlier, there is an important lesson to learn from the account of Samson and Delilah in the Old Testament (Judg. 16). The Philistines were enemies and they could not kill Samson with swords or bows, but they found a door. The Bible says that Samson loved Delilah. He became so infatuated with her that he was vulnerable.

It was not Delilah's beauty that captivated. It was not even her sexuality that destroyed Samson. Samson had known beautiful women before. He had slept with prostitutes. It was not just sexual exercise that caused her to get a grip on this man. I'll call it the Delilah syndrome.

Beauty and sex appeal are not the areas to concentrate on. When you focus on the wrong areas, you don't get the right results. Society teaches you today that if you have the right hair, the right face, the right shape, the right clothes, and the right car, then you will get the right man. Then you expect that you will buy the right house, have the right children, live the right life and live happily ever after. That is simply not true. Life is not a fairy tale.

God put some things into the feminine spirit that a man needs more than anything God put on the feminine body. If a woman knows who she is on the inside, no matter what she looks like, she will have no problem being attractive to a man. If she knows her own self-worth, then when she comes before that man, he will receive her.

The enemy wants you to be so focused on your outer appearance that you won't recognize your inner beauty, your inner strength, your inner glory. Your real value cannot be bought, applied, added on, hung from your ears, or laid on your neck. Your real strength is more than outward apparel and adornment for men. This real thing that causes a man to need you so desperately he can't leave you is not what is on you, but what is in you.

You need to recognize what God has put in you. God, when He made the woman, didn't just decorate the outside. He decorated the inside of the woman. He put beauty in her spirit.

The Scriptures talk about not having the outward adornment of gold, silver, and costly array. The Church took that passage and made a legal doctrine out of it. It was declared that there could be no jewelry, no makeup and no clothing of certain types. We are so negative at times. We were so busy dealing with the negative that we didn't hear the positive of what God said. God said that He had adorned the woman inwardly.

"Likewise, ye wives, be in subjection to your own husbands" (1 Pet. 3:1a). Notice that it didn't say women are to be subject to all men, just to her own husband. God did not make you a servant to all men. You have the right to choose who you will be in subjection to—and please choose very carefully. "That, if any obey not the word, they also may without the word be won by the conversation of the wives" (1 Pet. 3:1b).

Understand that the word *conversation* there refers to life style. You will not win him through lip-service; you will win him through your life style. He will see how you are, not what you say. He will watch how you act. He will watch your attitude. He will watch your disposition. A real problem for women believers today is that with the same mouth they use to witness to their husbands, they often curse others. You cannot witness to and win a man while he sits up and listens to you gossip about others.

"While they behold your chaste conversation [life style] coupled with fear" (1 Pet. 3:2). It didn't say anything about your ruby red lips or your long 25-dollar eyelashes. He should behold your life style, your chaste life style. *Chaste* is a word that means pure. Wives can win a husband by reverencing him.

*Whose adorning let it not be that outward adorning of plaiting the hair, and of wearing of gold, or of **putting on of apparel.*** 1 Peter 3:3

If that verse meant you could not wear these things, then it means you must be naked. Woman's beauty and strength are not on the outside. There is more to you than clothes. There's more to you than gold. There's more to you than hairdos.

Society promotes the notion that beauty is found in these outer things. However, if you keep working only on these outer things, you will find yourself looking in the mirror to find your value.

You could go broke fixing up the outside and still be lonely and alone. You need to understand that what brought Samson to Delilah so much he couldn't get up, was she became a place where he could rest. He laid on her and slept. The man was tired. She gave him rest. He needed it so desperately that even though he knew she was trying to kill him, he couldn't stay away.

If satan can work Delilah's strengths against men, then God can use them for men. If you are married, you can enrich your marriage through inner beauty. If you're not married, when you do get married, you'll understand it's not the necklaces you wear that make you attractive. It's not the twists you put in your hair. It's something that God puts in your heart that actually affects the man.

"But let it be the hidden man of the heart, in that which is not corruptible, even the *ornament of a meek and quiet spirit,* which is in the sight of God of great price" (1Pet. 3:4). God gave you the ornament of a meek and quiet spirit that is more valuable than any other outer form of jewelry. It is worth more than gold. It is more powerful than sexual ability.

When Samson hit Delilah's lap, she calmed him. Can you see what made Adam partake of the forbidden fruit, knowing it was evil? The Bible says Eve was deceived, but he knew. Do you see how powerful your influence is? The enemy wants to capitalize on what God put in you. That is why you must watch what goes through your doors.

"For after this manner in the old time the holy women also, who trusted in God, adorned themselves..." (1 Pet. 3:5). This is how they decorated themselves in the times of the partriarchs. Sarah was beautiful because she exhibited inner beauty and lived in obedience to Abraham. "Even as Sarah obeyed Abraham, calling him lord; whose daughters ye are, as long as ye do well, and are not afraid with any amazement" (1 Pet. 3:6).

You are Sarah's daughters when you are not afraid with any amazement. When you resist the temptation to react to circumstances and maintain a peaceful, meek and quiet spirit in times of frustration, then you are Sarah's daughters.

Jesus called the infirm woman. He unleashed a daughter of Abraham. If you can stay calm in a storm, if you can praise God under pressure, if you can worship in the midst of critics and criticism, God says you are Sarah's daughter.

If you can keep a calm head when the bills are more than the income, and not lose control when satan says you won't make it, if you can stand in the midst of the storm, you are Sarah's daughter.

If you can rebuke the fear that is knocking at the door of your heart, and tell that low self-esteem it cannot come in, and rebuke all the spirits that are waiting to attack you and make you captive, you are Sarah's daughter.

If you can stand calm in the midst of the storm and say, "I know God will deliver me," you are Sarah's daughter. If you can walk with God in the midst of the storm and trust Him to bring you through dry places, you are Sarah's daughter.

If you can judge God faithful, and know that God cannot lie, understanding that satan is the father of lies, you are Sarah's daughter.

If you can stand there when fear is trying to get you to overreact and fall apart, you are Sarah's daughter. If you can stand there and push a tear from off the side of your face and smile in the middle of the rain, you are Sarah's daughter.

God is adorning you with glory, power and majesty. He will send people into your life to appreciate your real beauty, your real essence. It is the kind of beauty that lasts in a face full of wrinkles, gray hair, falling arches, crow's feet, and all the pitfalls that may come your way. There's a beauty that you can see in a 90-year-old woman's face that causes an old man to smile. God is decorating you on the inside. He is putting a glory in you that will shine through your eyes. A man will come along and look in your eyes. He will not talk about whether they were blue or whether your eye-shadow was right or not. He will look in your eyes and see trust, peace, love and life.

Appreciate the ornaments of God. Let God give you a new attitude. Let Him wash everything out of your spirit that is against Him. Let go of anger, hate, frustration and bitterness. God wants you unleashed. He repeats today, just as He did two thousand years ago, "Woman, thou art loosed."

Beauty comes in many ways. However, true beauty is always on the inside. A faithful wife is more precious than words can express. The inner beauty that makes you valuable to God will also make you valuable to others. Some may take just longer to notice it. Regardless of how long it takes, know the attractiveness and beauty that is within.

Perhaps you feel scared by the past. Maybe you think you are unattractive and unworthy. Nothing could be more untrue. God painted a wonderful piece of artwork one day. That painting is you.

*C*hapter 13

EVERY WOMAN NEEDS A SABBATH

We have dealt with many aspects of the story of Jesus healing the infirm woman. However, in this chapter I would like to look at an issue underlying the miracle. It does not really concern either the woman or Christ. It is the time of healing: the Sabbath day.

The Sabbath is a day of rest. It is a day of restoration. Following creation, on the seventh day, God rested (Gen. 2:2). Rest is for the purpose of restoration. It is not just because you're tired. It is during a time of rest that you replenish or receive back those things that were expended or put out. It is during the time of restoration that the enemy wants to break off your fellowship with the Lord.

I don't want you to think of rest just in terms of sleep. Please understand that rest and restoration are related concepts. The enemy does not want you to have rest. You need calmness or Sabbath rest because it is through the resting of your spirit that the restoration of your life begins to occur.

It is not a mere coincidence that this woman was healed on the Sabbath day. The Bible goes to great pains to make us aware that it was during the Sabbath that this woman experienced her healing. The Sabbath was meant not only for God to rest, but also for God to enjoy His creation with man. The issues are rest and communion.

In the nation of Israel, God used the Sabbath day as a sign of the covenant. It proved that they were His people. They spent time in worship and fellowship with the Lord. That is the Sabbath. It is real communion between the heart of man and heart of God.

When Jesus began to minister in a restful situation, needs began to be manifested. The infirm woman's need was revealed in the midst of the Sabbath. You can never get your needs met by losing your head. When you calm down, God speaks.

When you start murmuring and complaining, the only thing God can focus on is your unbelief. When you start resting in Him, He can focus on your problems and on the areas of your life that need to be touched.

When you begin to enter into real worship with God, that's the best time to have Him minister to your needs. That's the time God does restoration in your life. Satan, therefore, wants to break up your Sabbath rest.

Jesus healed this woman on the Sabbath. One thing you can't seem to deliver religious people from is their being religious. Sometimes I would rather deal with rank sinners than with religious people. They esteem religiosity above God's creation. They are more concerned about keeping doctrine than about helping people. Man is God's concern above everything else.

The infirm woman was not sitting around complaining. She was not murmuring. She was not hysterical. She had a problem, but she was calm. She was just sitting there listening to the words of the Master. She brought her problem with her, but her problem had not dominated her worship.

I want to zoom in on the Sabbath day because what the Sabbath was physically, Christ is spiritually. Christ is our Sabbath rest. He is the end of our labors. We are saved by grace through faith and not by works, lest any man should be able to boast (Eph. 2:8-9). Jesus said:

> *Come unto Me, all ye that labour and are heavy laden, and I will give you rest. Take My yoke upon you, and learn of Me; for I am meek and lowly in heart: and ye shall find rest unto your souls. For My yoke is easy, and My burden is light.* Matthew 11:28-30

The rest of the Lord is so complete that when Jesus was dying on the cross, He said, "It is finished" (Jn. 19:30). It was so powerful. For the first time in history, a high priest sat down in the presence of God without having to run in and out bringing blood to atone the sins of man.

When Christ entered in once and for all, He offered up Himself for us that we might be delivered from sin.

If you really want to be healed, you've got to be in Him. If you really want to be set free, and experience restoration, you've got to be in Him, because your healing comes in the Sabbath rest. Your healing comes in Christ Jesus. As you rest in Him, every infirmity, every area bent out of place will be restored.

The devil knows this truth, so he does not want you to rest in the Lord. Satan wants you to be anxious. He wants you to be upset. He wants you to be hysterical. He wants you to be suicidal, doubtful, fearful and neurotic.

> *There remaineth therefore a rest to the people of God. For he that is entered into His rest, he also hath ceased from his own works, as God did from His. Let us labour therefore to enter into that rest, lest any man fall after the same example of unbelief.* Hebrews 4:9-11

Sometimes it takes work to find the place of rest and calm. Our hectic world does not lend itself to quiet and peace. It creates noise and uneasiness. Even though the infirm woman was bowed over and could not lift herself, she rested in the fact that she was in the presence of a mighty God. He is able to do exceedingly and abundantly above all that we may ask or think (Eph. 3:20).

Jesus also confronted the woman at the well with some exciting truths.

Jesus answered and said unto her, Whosoever drinketh of this water shall thirst again: but whosoever drinketh of the water that I shall give him shall never thirst; but the water that I shall give him shall be in him a well of water springing up into everlasting life. John 4:13-14

Jesus was sitting at the well waiting for someone to return. He was relaxed. He was calm and resting. He knew who He was. God doesn't get excited about circumstances.

Another time the disciples and Jesus were on a ship. The storm arose and appeared to be about to sink the ship. However, Jesus didn't become concerned about circumstances. In fact, He was sleeping, resting in the middle of a crisis. Everyone else was running all over the boat trying to figure out how they would get into life jackets and into the lifeboats. Was Jesus resting because He was lazy? No, He was resting because He knew He was greater than the storm. Jesus rose up and spoke to the winds and waves and said, "Peace, be still" (Mk. 4:39).

When you know who you are, you don't have to struggle. You don't have to work Him up.

That was Christ's attitude when the woman at the well met Him. When this woman came down with her waterpot on her shoulder, she was all upset and worried about the water she needed to draw. Jesus was sitting by the well. He began to demonstrate calmness. He told her, "If you drink of the water that you have, you will thirst again, but if you drink of the water that I have, you will never thirst."

> *The woman saith unto Him, Sir, give me this*
> *water, that I thirst not, neither come hither to*
> *draw. Jesus saith unto her, Go, call thy hus-*
> *band, and come hither.* John 4:15-16

Jesus shifted the focus of the conversation to the real need.

> *The woman answered and said, I have no hus-*
> *band. Jesus said unto her, Thou hast well said,*
> *I have no husband: for thou hast had five hus-*
> *bands; and he whom thou now hast is not thy*
> *husband: in that saidst thou truly.* John 4:17-18

Like this woman, you can get yourself into situations that wound and upset your spirit. These kinds of wounds can't be healed through human effort. You must get in the presence of God and let Him fill those voids in your life. You will not settle it up by going from friend to friend. This woman had already tried that. She had already gone through five men. The answer is not getting another man. It's getting in touch with *the Man—Jesus.*

The woman at the well threw down her waterpot and ran to tell others about the man she had met at the well. We too need to get rid of the old, carnal man. Some of those old attachments and old ways of living need to be replaced with the calmness of the Spirit.

This woman could never have rid herself of the old man until she met the new man. When you meet the new, you get the power to say good-bye to the old. You will never be able to break the grip on your life that those old ways have until you know Jesus Christ is the real way. You will never get it straight without Jesus. You must come to Him just as you are. Knowing Him will give you the power to break away from the old self and the ties that bind.

If you have something that has attached itself to you that is not of God, you won't be able to break it through your own strength. Submit yourself unto God, resist the enemy, and he will flee from you (Jas. 4:7). As you submit to God, you receive the power to resist the enemy.

This woman didn't even go back home. She ran into the city telling everyone to come and see the Man who had told her about her life. You do yourself a disservice until you really come to know Jesus. He satisfies. Everyone else, well, they pacify, but Jesus satisfies. He can satisfy every need and every yearning. He heals every pain and every affliction. Then He lifts every burden and every trouble in your life.

You have had enough tragedy. You have been bent over long enough. God will do something good in you. God kept you living through all those years of infirmity because He had something greater for you than what you've experienced earlier. God kept you because He has something better for you.

You may have been abused and misused. Perhaps all those you trusted in turned on you and broke your heart. Still God has sustained you. You didn't make it because you were strong. You didn't make it because you were smart. You didn't make it because you were wise. You made it because God's amazing grace kept you and sustained you. God has more for you today than what you went through yesterday. Don't give up. Don't give in. Hold on. The blessing is on the way.

I dare you to realize that you can do all things through Christ who strengthens you (Phil. 4:13). Once the infirm woman knew that she didn't have to be bent over, she stood straight up. Jesus told the woman at the well to get rid of the old. He wanted her to step away from that old pattern of selfishness. Suddenly, she recognized that she didn't have what she thought she had. The sinful things that you have fought to maintain are not worth what you thought they were.

I'm referring to some of those things that have attached themselves to your life in which you find comfort. Some of those habits you have come to enjoy, some of those relationships you thought you found security in, were not profitable. Often we settle for less because we didn't meet the best. When you get the best, it gives you the power to let go of the rest.

The infirm woman didn't panic because of her crippling disease. She had been in torment and pain for 18 years. When she came into the presence of Jesus, she relaxed in Him. She expected that He would take care of her. The result was a wonderful healing. The woman at the well expected water, but left the well having found the Savior. She sought temporal satisfaction, but found eternal satisfaction.

That's what rest and Sabbath is. It is the ability to find eternal satisfaction in Jesus. The world will never give us peace and satisfaction. Jesus offers both freely.

The woman who has struggled can find satisfaction. You can find hope for your soul. It is found in the Master of the universe. He will not deny you because of your past. He will not scrutinize your every action. He will take you as you are and give you rest. He will provide a peace that will satisfy the very yearning of your soul.

And the peace of God, which passeth all understanding, shall keep your hearts and minds through Christ Jesus. Philippians 4:7

the well expected water, but left the well having found the Savior. She sought temporal satisfaction, but found eternal satisfaction.

That's what rest and Sabbath is. It is the ability to find eternal satisfaction in Jesus. The world will never give us peace and satisfaction. Jesus offers both freely.

The woman who has struggled can find satisfaction. You can find hope for your soul. It is found in the Master of the universe. He will not deny you because of your past. He will not scrutinize your every action. He will take you as you are and give you rest. He will provide a peace that will satisfy the very yearning of your soul

And the peace of God, which passeth all understanding, shall keep your hearts and minds through Christ Jesus. Philippians 4:7

Chapter 14

WINTER WOMAN

*And she said unto them, Call me not Naomi,
call me Mara: for the Almighty hath dealt very
bitterly with me. I went out full, and the Lord
hath brought me home again empty: why then
call ye me Naomi, seeing the Lord hath testi-
fied against me, and the Almighty hath afflicted me?* Ruth 1:20-21

This morning when I rose, the land was still asleep. I
watched the miracle of beginnings from the veranda of
my hotel. The waves of the sea wandered listlessly in and
dashed themselves on empty beaches where the sand
smiled at the peacefulness of the breaking day. Like the
initial sounds of an orchestra warming up for a concerto,
the sea gulls cried and screeched out their opening solos.
The wind watched, occasionally brushing past the palm
trees spreading their leaves like the fan of a distinguished
lady. Far to the east the sun creeped up on stage as if it
was trying to arrive without disturbing anyone. It peeked

up over the ocean like the eye of a child around a corner as he stealthily plays peek-a-boo.

If I had not stayed perched on my window's edge, I would have misjudged the day. I would have thought that the morning or perhaps the bustling sun-drenched after-noon was the most beautiful part of the day. I would have thought the sound of laughing, hysterically happy chil-dren running into or away from the ocean would, without contention, have won the award for the best part of the day. But just before I turned in my ballot and cast my vote in the poll, the wisdom of the evening slipped up on the stage. The early morning entertainment and the bustling sounds of the afternoon had distracted me. Now I looked over in the distance as the sun began its descent. I noticed that the crescendo of the concert is always reserved for the closing. How had I not noticed that the sun had changed her sundress to an evening gown, full of color and grandeur. The grace of a closing day is far greater than the uncertainty of morning. The next time you get a chance to notice a sun burst into its neon rainbow and curtsy before setting in the west, you will scratch out your early scrib-bling and recast your vote; for the most beautiful part of the day, in fact the most beautiful part of a woman's life, is at the setting of the sun.

I write this with my mother in mind. Her hair has changed colors before my eyes. Like afterthoughts of an artist, lines have been etched upon her brow. Her arms are much weaker now and her gait much slower; but she is somehow warmer at life's winter age than she was in the summer days. All of life's tragedy has been wrestled to the mat and still she stands to attest to the authenticity of her goals, dreams and ambitions. What is wrong with hanging around the stage to collect an encore from a grateful audience whose lives have been touched by the beauty of your song? Just because the glare of summer doesn't beat upon your face doesn't mean that there is nothing left for you to do. Whose presence will stand as a witness that God will see you through? Who will care to catch a glimpse of your children run their race or catch them when they fall beneath the weight of their day? God never extends days beyond purpose. My daughters are in their springtime, my wife is in the middle of summer, and my mother is walking through autumn to step into winter. Together they form a chord of womanhood—three different notes creating a harmonious blend. To the reader, I would suggest: Enjoy every note.

> *While the earth remaineth, seedtime and harvest, and cold and heat, and summer and winter, and day and night shall not cease.*
> Genesis 8:22

Our culture has celebrated youth to such a degree that we have isolated the elderly. The Hollywood mentality accentuates the dynamics of youth as though each season of life didn't have its own beauty. Anyone who observes nature will tell you that all seasons have their own advantages and disadvantages. It is important that we teach women to prepare for the winter. I believe age can be stressful for women in a way that it isn't for men— only because we have not historically recognized women at other stages in their lives. Equally disturbing is the fact that statisticians tell us women tend to live longer, more productive lives than their male counterparts. It is not their longevity of life that is disturbing; it is the fact that many times, because of an early death of their spouse, they have no sense of companionship.

The Bible admonishes us to minister to the widows. Little instruction is given in regard to the care of aged men. We need to invest some effort in encouraging older women. They have a need for more than just provision of natural substance. Many women spend their lives building their identity around their role rather than around their person. When the role changes, they feel somewhat displaced. Because being a good mother is a self-sacrificing job, when those demands have subsided, many women feel like Naomi. Her name meant "my joy." But after losing her children and husband she said, "Change my name to 'Mara'." Mara means "bitterness." Don't allow changing times to change who you are. It is dan-gerous to lose your identity in your circumstances. Circumstances change and when they do, the older woman can feel empty and unfulfilled. In spite of Naomi's bout with depression, God still had much for her to contribute. So just because the demands have changed, that doesn't mean your life is over. Redefine your pur-pose, gather your assets and keep on living and giving. As long as you can maintain a sense of worth, you can resist the "Mara" mentality.

Naomi was a collection of tragedies. She had weath-ered many storms. Discouragement comes when people feel they have seen it all and most of it was really terrible! No matter what age you are, you have never seen it all. There are no graduations from the school of life other than

death. No one knows how God will end His book, but He

does tend to save the best for last. Israel didn't recognize Jesus because they were so used to seeing what they had already seen. God had sent dozens of prophets, and when He finally sends a king, they failed to recognize Him. It is dangerous to assume that what you will see out of life will be similar to what you saw before. God has the strangest way of restoring purpose to your life. For Naomi, it was through a relationship she tried to dissuade. It is dangerous to keep sending people away. The very one you are trying to send away may have the key to restoring purpose and fulfillment to your life.

> *And Ruth said, Entreat me not to leave thee, or to return from following after thee: for whither thou goest, I will go; and where thou lodgest, I will lodge: thy people shall be my people, and thy God my God. Ruth 1:16*

Ruth was Naomi's daughter-in-law. Naomi thought their only connection was her now dead son. Many times we, who have been very family-oriented, do not understand friendships. When family circumstances change, we lapse into isolation because we know nothing of other relationships. There are bonds that are stronger than blood (see Prov. 18:24). They are God-bonds! When God brings someone into our life, He is the bonding agent. Ruth said, "Your God shall be my God." God wanted Naomi to see the splendor of winter relationships, the joy of passing the baton of her wisdom and strength to someone worthy of her attention. Let God choose such a person for us because too often we choose on the basis of fleshly ties and not godly ties. I have noticed in the Scriptures that the strongest female relationships tend to be exemplified between older and younger women. I am certainly not suggesting that such will always be the case. However, let me submit a few cases for your own edification.

1. Ruth would have died in Moab, probably marrying some heathenistic idolator if it were not for the wisdom of Naomi, an older, more seasoned woman. Naomi knew how to provide guidance without manipulation—a strength many women at that stage of life do not have. Ruth was, of course, one of the great-grandparents in the lineage of Jesus Christ. She had greatness in her that God used Naomi to cultivate. Perhaps Naomi would have been called Mara and perhaps she would have ended up dying in bitterness instead of touching lives if it had not been for Ruth.

2. Elisabeth, the wife of the priest Zacharias, is the biblical synonym for the modern pastor's wife. She was a winter woman with a summer experience. She was pregnant with a promise. In spite of her declining years, she was fulfilling more destiny then than she had in her youth. She is biblical proof that God blesses us in His own time and on His own terms. She is also in seclusion. Perhaps it was the attitude of the community. Many times when an older woman is still vibrant and productive it can cause jealousy and intimidation. Perhaps it was the silent stillness in her womb which some believe she experienced. Whatever the reason, she was a recluse

for six months until she heard a knock at the door. If you have isolated yourself from others, regardless of the reason, I pray you will hear the knocking of the Lord. He will give you the garment of praise to clothe the spirit of heaviness (Is. 61:3).

When Elisabeth lifted her still-creaking body, which seemed almost anchored down to the chair, and drug her enlarged torso to the door, she saw a young girl, a picture of herself in days gone by, standing there. Opening that door changed her life forever. As you open the door to new relationships and remove the chain from your own fears, God will overwhelm you with new splendor. Mary, the future mother of our Savior and Lord, Elisabeth's young cousin, was at the door. The salutation of this young woman, the exposure to her experience, made the baby in Elisabeth's womb leap and Elisabeth was filled with the Holy Ghost. God will jump-start your heart! He doesn't mean for you to go sit in a chair and die! *In Jesus' name, get up and answer the door!* People probably wondered why these women were so close who were so different, but it was a God-bond!

While I was in school, I worked at a local paint store. I had to acquaint myself with the products and procedures. I was intrigued by a refinishing product that restored old furniture to its former luster. I purchased the product to see if it was as effective as I had been told. I learned right away that the most difficult part of restoring furniture was stripping off the old wax. It takes patience to overcome the effects of years of use and abuse. If you are not committed to getting back what you once had, you could easily decide that the process is impossible. Nevertheless, I assure you it is not impossible. David, the psalmist, declares, "He restoreth my soul" (Ps. 23:3). The term *restoreth* is a process. Only God knows what it takes to remove the build-up that may be existing in your life. But He specializes in restoring and renewing the human heart.

> And the women said unto Naomi, Blessed be the Lord, which hath not left thee this day without a kinsman, that his name may be famous in Israel. And he shall be unto thee a restorer of thy life, and a nourisher of thine old age: for thy daughter in law, which loveth thee, which is better to thee than seven sons, hath born him. Ruth 4:14-15

Naomi almost changed her name to Mara. She felt that God had dealt very bitterly with her. It is dangerous to be prejudiced against God. Prejudice is to pre-judge. People, even believers, have often prejudged God. However, He isn't finished yet. Before it was over, everyone agreed that the hand of the Lord was upon Naomi. Therefore, you are not off course. Trust Him to see you through days that may be different from the ones you encountered earlier. You are being challenged with the silent struggles of winter. I believe the most painful experience is to look backward and have to stare into the cold face of regret. Most people have thought, "I wonder how things would have been had I not made this decision or that one." To realize that you have been the victim and the assailant in your own life may be difficult to accept—especially since most of those dilemmas are birthed through the womb of your own decisions. Admittedly, there are those who inadvertently crashed into circumstances that stripped them, wounded them and left them feeling like the victim on the Jericho road! No matter which case best describes your current situation, first pause and thank God that, like Naomi, in spite of the tragedies of youth, it is a miracle that you survived the solemn chill of former days. Your presence should be a praise. Look over your shoulder and see what could have been. Has God dealt with you bitterly? I think not.

Anyone can recognize Him in the sunshine, but in the storm His disciples thought He was a ghost (Mt. 14:26). There are two things every Naomi can rely upon as she gathers wood for winter days and wraps quilts around weak, willowy legs: (a) God is a restorer. That is to say, as you sit by the fire sipping coffee, rehearsing your own thoughts, playing old reruns from the scenes in your life—some things He will explain and others He will heal. Restoration doesn't mean all the lost people who left you will return. Neither Naomi's husband nor her sons were resurrected. It is just that God gives purpose back to the years that had question marks. How many times have you been able to look back and say, "If I hadn't gone through that, I wouldn't have known or received this." Simply said, "He'll make it up to you." He restores the effects of the years of turmoil. People who heard Naomi running through the house with rollers in her hair complaining that God had dealt bitterly, should have waited with their noses pressed against the window pane as God masterfully brought peace into her arms. If you wait by the window, you will hear the soft hum of an old woman nodding with her grandchild clutched in her arms. Perhaps she is too proud to tell you that she charged God foolishly, but the smile on her leathery face and the calmness of her rest says, "He doeth all things well" (Mk. 7:37).

And I will restore to you the years that the locust hath eaten, the cankerworm, and the caterpillar, and the palmerworm, my great army which I sent among you. And ye shall eat in plenty, and be satisfied, and praise the name of the Lord your God, that hath dealt wondrously with you: and My people shall never be ashamed. Joel 2:25-26

The Lord will be known as: (b) the nourisher. This may be a difficult role for you who have clutched babies and men alike to the warm breast of your sensitivity. You, who have been the source for others to be strengthened, may find it difficult to know what to do with this role reversal. The nourisher must learn to be nourished. Many women pray more earnestly as intercessors for others than for themselves. That is wonderful, but there ought to be a time that you desire certain things for yourself. Our God is El Shaddai, "the breasted one" (from Gen. 17:1). He gives strength to the feeble and warmth to the cold. There is great comfort in His arms. Like children, even adults can snuggle into His everlasting arms and hear the heartbeat of a loving God who says, "And ye shall eat in plenty, and be satisfied, and praise the name of your God..." (Joel 2:26).

Expect God in all His varied forms. He is a master of disguise, a guiding star in the night, a lily left growing in the valley, or an answered prayer sent on the breath of an angel. Angels are the butlers of Heaven; they open doors. He sends angels to minister to His own. Have you ever seen an angel? They aren't always dressed in white with dramatically arched wings. Sometimes they are so ordinary that they can be overlooked. Ruth was an angel that Naomi almost sent away. God can use anyone as a channel of nourishment. Regardless of the channel, He is still the source.

> *Do not forget to entertain strangers, for by so doing some people have entertained angels without knowing it.* Hebrews 13:2 (NIV)

When Hagar was lost in the wilderness of depression and wrestling exasperation, God sent an angel. When the labor-ridden mother of Samson was mundane and barren, God sent an angel. When young Mary was wandering listlessly through life, God sent an angel. When the grief-stricken Mary Magdalene came stumbling down to the tomb, God sent an angel. For every woman in crises, there is an angel! For every lonely night and forgotten mother, there is an angel. For every lost young girl wandering the concrete jungle of an inner city, there is an angel. My sister, set your coffee down, take the blanket off your legs, and stand up on your feet! Hast thou not known, hast thou not heard? For every woman facing winter, *there is an angel!*

Are not all angels ministering spirits sent to serve those who will inherit salvation?
Hebrews 1:14 (NIV)

Through faith also Sarah herself received strength to conceive seed, and was delivered of a child when she was past age, because she judged Him faithful who had promised.
Hebrews 11:11

I think it would be remiss of me not to share, before moving on, the miracles of winter. In the summer, all was well with Sarah. At that time she knew little about Jehovah, her husband's God. She basically knew she was in love with a wonderful man. She was the luckiest woman in Ur. An incredibly beautiful woman already, she wore her love like a striking woman wears a flattering dress. The air smelled like honeysuckle and the wind called her name. Then her husband spoke to her about moving. Where, she didn't know, and crazy as it may sound to those who have forgotten the excitement of summer, she really didn't care. She ran into the tent and began to pack. Sometimes it's good to get away from relatives and friends. Starting over would be fun!

Soon the giddy exuberance of summer started to ebb as she began wrestling with the harsh realities of following a dreamer. Abraham had not done what he said; he carried a few of their relatives with them. "I am sure he had a good reason," she thought. What was really troubling her wasn't the strife between the relatives or the fighting herdsmen, it was the absence of a child. By now she was sure she was barren. She felt like she had cheated

Abraham out of an important part of life. Someone had said she would have a baby. Sarah laughed, "If I am going to get a miracle, God had better hurry." I want to warn you against setting your own watch. God's time is not your time. He may not come when you want Him to, but He is right on time. Twice it is mentioned that Sarah laughed. The first time she laughed at God; in the winter time she laughed with God. The first time she laughed at the impossibility of God's promise. After she had gone through life's experiences, she learned that God is faithful to perform His word.

THE FIRST LAUGH

> *Abraham and Sarah were already old and well advanced in years, and Sarah was past the age of childbearing. So Sarah laughed to herself as she thought, "After I am worn out and my master is old, will I now have this pleasure?" Then the Lord said to Abraham, "Why did Sarah laugh and say, 'Will I really have a child, now that I am old?' Is anything too hard for the Lord? I will return to you at the appointed time next year and Sarah will have a son."* Genesis 18:11-14 (NIV)

THE LAST LAUGH

> *Sarah became pregnant and bore a son to Abraham in his old age, at the very time God had promised him. Abraham gave the name Isaac to the son Sarah bore him. When his son Isaac was eight days old, Abraham circumcised him,*

171

as God commanded him. Abraham was a hun-
dred years old when his son Isaac was born to
him. Sarah said, "God has brought me laugh-
ter, and everyone who hears about this will
laugh with me." And she added, "Who would
have said to Abraham that Sarah would nurse
children? Yet I have borne him a son in his old
age." Genesis 21:2-7 (NIV)

Listen carefully at what I am about to say. It is rele-
vant to you. I am not so much concerned with the eigh-
teenth chapter of Genesis where she laughs in unbelief.
Nor am I focusing my attention on the twenty-first chapter where she laughs with "the joy of the Lord." I want to
discuss with you the events that led to the miracles of her
winter. Often we share our personal testimony. We tell
where we started and even where we ultimately arrived,
without sharing the process or the sequence of events that
led to our deliverance. Then our listeners feel defeated
because they named it and claimed it and still didn't
attain it! We didn't tell them about the awful trying of our
faith that preceded our coming forth as pure gold. Today,
however, we will share the whole truth and nothing but
the truth! Amen.

In between these powerful moments in the life of one
of God's finest examples of wives, everything in her was
tested. I believe that her love for Abram gave her the
courage to leave home, but her love for God brought forth
the promised seed. Careful now, I am not saying that her
love for God replaced her love for her husband; I am
merely saying that it complemented the other to the high-
est level. After all, what good is it to appreciate what God

gave us if we do not appreciate the God who gave it to us? If age should do nothing else, it should help us put things in proper perspective. There is nothing like time to show us that we have misplaced priorities.

In summer, she followed Abram out of their country and away from their kindred. As the seasons of life changed, she takes another pilgrimage into what could have been a great tragedy. Abraham, her beloved husband, leads his wife into Gerar. As I am a man and a leader myself, I dare not be too hard on him. Anyone can make a poor decision. The decision to go to Gerar I could defend, even though Gerar means "halting place." I have made decisions that brought me to a halting place in my life. What's reprehensible is that Abraham, Sarah's protector and covering, when afraid for his own safety, lied about her identity (Gen. 20). You never know who people are until you witness them under pressure. Now, I am not being sanctimonious about Abraham's flagrant disregard for truth. But it was a life-threatening lie.

Have you ever known someone upon whom you had cast the weight of your confidence, only to have your trust defrauded in a moment of self-gratification and indulgence? Someone who has a selfish need can jeopardize all that you have. Abraham's infamous lie jeopardized the safety of his wife. King Abimelech was a heathen king. He was used to getting whatever he wanted. His reputation for debauchery preceded him to the degree that Abraham, the father of faith, feared for his life. Rather than risk himself, he told the king that his lovely wife was really his sister. Abraham knew that such a statement would cause Sarah to have to fulfill the torrid desires of a heathenist. Sarah now finds herself being bathed and perfumed to be offered up as an offering of lust for the passions of the king. Imagine the icy grip of fear clutching the first lady of faith. Imagine her shock to realize that under real stress, a person can never be sure what another individual will do to secure his own well-being. Her Abraham failed her. But God did not! Maybe there is someone in your life who selfishly threw you into a tempestuous situation. Take courage! Just because satan has set a snare doesn't mean you can't escape. The God we serve is able. His word to you is, "Woman, thou art loosed."

Abraham's faith had always been the star of the Old Testament, but not that day. It's amazing how faith will come up in your heart at a crisis. Consider Sarah. She is facing the anxious footsteps of her rapist. She knows it will not be long until she will be abused. Like a frightened rabbit crouched in a corner, she realizes Abraham will not rescue her. I don't know what she prayed, but I know she cried out to the only One she had left! Maybe she said, "God of Abraham, I need you to be my God too. Save me from this pending fate." Or maybe she just cried, "O God! Have mercy on me!" Whatever she said, God heard her. He will hear you as well. You don't have time to be angry or bitter. You've just got enough time to pray. Call out to Him. He is your God too!

God shut up all the wombs in the king's household. He spoke up for Sarah when no one else would. He threatened the king and revealed the truth. "She is Abraham's wife," declared God! He stopped the footsteps of danger! Very few men understand a woman's terror of being raped or sexually assaulted. I can only imagine the tears that ran down her face when she heard the door open. Her would-be rapist comes in, falls to the floor and begins to cry out, "He touched me!" Did you know that the heart of the king is in His hand and He turneth it as He will! (Prov. 21:1)

When Sarah came out of Gerar, she knew something about life, about people, and most of all, about God. She didn't lose her relationship with Abraham, as we will soon see. But she did learn something that all of us must learn too. She learned the faithfulness of God. I am convinced that the things that worry us would not, if we knew the faithfulness of God. Have you ever spent the night in a Gerar situation? If you have, you know the Lord in a way you could never know Him otherwise. He cares for you! Look over your past and remember His faithfulness. Look at your future and trust Him now!

Right after this nightmare experience, the Bible says in Genesis 21:1-2, "And the Lord visited Sarah as He had said, and the Lord did unto Sarah as He had spoken. For Sarah conceived, and bare Abraham a son in his old age, at the set time of which God had spoken to him." It wasn't Abraham's visit to the tent that left that woman filled with the promise of God. Without God he could do nothing. Always remember that man may be the instrument, but God is the life source. It was God who visited Sarah. Now Sarah knew God like she had never known Him. Some things you can learn about God only in the winter. Sarah won a spot in the hallmark of faith. When Hebrews chapter 11 lists the patriarchs and their awesome faith, this winter woman's name is included. Abraham is mentioned for the kind of faith that would leave home and look for a city whose builder and maker is God (v. 10). But when it comes to discussing the kind of faith that caused an old woman's barren womb to conceive, it was Sarah's faith that did it. She didn't take faith classes. She just went through her winter clutching the warm hand of a loving God who would not fail. So when you hear Sarah laughing the last time, she is laughing with God. She is holding her baby to her now wrinkled breast. She understands the miracles that come only to winter women.

Chapter 15

BREAKING THE CHAIN

There is awesome power in women. God has chosen that women serve as the vehicles through which entry is made into this world. He has shared His creativity with women. Women are strong and willing to nurture others.

In spite of this, millions of women continually suffer emotional, physical, and spiritual strain. The enemy has attempted to destroy God's vehicle of creativity.

You may be one of those who suffer. Perhaps you sit and wonder whether life will ever be normal for you. Maybe you feel like your circumstance has made you different from other women. You feel like you are alone, with no one to help you find healing.

It could be that your emotional strain comes from having been abused. Others have taken advantage of you and used you in the most horrible and depraved ways. You are left feeling used and dirty. How could anyone want someone who has been abused? Nevertheless, you are wanted. God wants you, and God's people want you.

Mistakes made early in life impact the rest of our lives. Some become involved sexually without the commitment of marriage. Maybe you believed him when he told you that he loved you. Perhaps you really did think that yielding would show your true love. Or, maybe, you simply wanted to have a good time without thinking about the consequences. You too feel less than normal.

God has determined your need. He looked down from Heaven and saw your pain and guilt. He evaluated the situation and decided that you needed a Redeemer. You need Someone to reach down and lift you. He saw that you needed to recognize how important you are. It is impossible to know all that was in the mind of God when He looked down on broken humanity, but we know He looked past our broken hearts, wounded histories, and our tendency to sin, and saw our need.

He met that need through Jesus Christ. Jesus took your abuse on Himself on the cross of Calvary. He paid for your shame. He made a way for you to be clean again. He took your indiscretions and sins upon Himself and died in your place. He saw your desire to please others and feel good. Thus, He took all your sinful desires and crucified them on the cross.

When you accept Him, you become clean and holy. You are made pure. Don't think you were alone, though; everyone struggles with the same kinds of sins as you, whether they show it on the outside or not.

The abused little girl with all her wounds was healed by the stripes of Jesus (Is. 53:5). The sins of the woman who wanted to fulfill her lusts was crucified on the cross with Him (Gal. 2:20). The past is paid for. The wounds may leave scars, but the scars are only there to remind us that we are human. Everyone has scars.

God recognizes the possibility of what you can become. He has a plan. He sees your potential. He also knows that your potential has been bound by your history. Your suffering made you into a different woman from the one He originally intended you to be. The circumstances of life shaped your way of thinking. The responses you made to those circumstances often kept you from living up to your potential.

God knows that there is a Sarah, a Rahab, a woman at the well, a Ruth, or even a Mary in you. Hidden inside of you is a great woman who can do great exploits in His name. He wants that woman to be set free. He wants the potential within you to be unleashed so you can become the person you were created to be.

There is only one way to reach that potential. He is calling you. He will spiritually stir your heart and let you know that He is moving in your life, if you will only respond to His call.

The power to unleash you is in your faith. Dare to believe that He will do what He said He would do. Shift your confidence from your own weaknesses to His power. Trust in Him rather than in yourself. Anyone who comes to Christ will find deliverance and healing. He will soothe your wounds. He will comfort you in your desperate moments. He will raise you up.

Believe that He paid the price for your sin and guilt. Believe that He has washed you and made you clean. Believe that He will satisfy every need created by your history. Have faith that He will reward you when you call on Him and it shall be done.

You have nothing to lose, and everything to gain. Jesus will straighten the crooked places in your heart and make you completely whole. When you allow Him access to every area of your life, you will never be the same broken person again.

> *Therefore, if anyone is in Christ [s]he is a new creation; the old has gone, the new has come!*
> 2 Corinthians 5:17 (NIV)

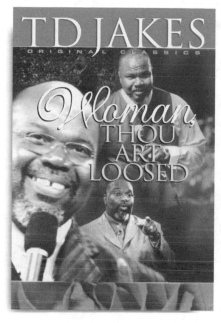

Best-Selling Author
T.D. Jakes

WOMAN, THOU ART LOOSED GIFT SET

With words that stand the test of time, T.D. Jakes' three books cross denominational lines, racial barriers, and gender biases to reach into the heart of the reader. With the compassion of Jesus Christ, he touches the hidden places of every woman's heart to bring healing to past wounds with the phenomenal best-selling *Woman, Thou Art Loosed!* With the same intensity he calls all men, women, and children to stop being afraid to reveal what God longs to heal in *Naked and Not Ashamed.* Only when we drop our masks and facades can we be real before our Lord and others. And with *Can You Stand to Be Blessed?* T.D. Jakes, a man of many accomplishments and life goals, shares personal insights that will help all people survive the peaks and valleys of daily living out God's call upon their lives. This classics gift set is sure to become a special part of every reader's personal library!
ISBN 0-7684-3036-4 (Boxed Gift Set)

Also Available Separately.

WOMAN, THOU ART LOOSED!
ISBN 0-7684-3040-2

CAN YOU STAND TO BE BLESSED?
ISBN 0-7684-3042-9

NAKED AND NOT ASHAMED
ISBN 0-7684-3041-0

Available at your local Christian bookstore.

www.destinyimage.com

Additional copies of this book and other book titles from DESTINY IMAGE are available at your local bookstore.

For a complete list of our titles, visit us at www.destinyimage.com Send a request for a catalog to:

Destiny Image₍ᵣ₎ Publishers, Inc.
P.O. Box 310
Shippensburg, PA 17257-0310

"Speaking to the Purposes of God for This Generation and for the Generations to Come"